SAY IT WITH MUSIC
The Story of Irving Berlin

SAY IT WITH MUSIC
The Story of Irving Berlin

Nancy Furstinger

**MORGAN
REYNOLDS**
Publishing, Inc.

620 South Elm Street, Suite 223
Greensboro, North Carolina   27406
http://www.morganreynolds.com

SAY IT WITH MUSIC: THE STORY OF IRVING BERLIN

Library of Congress Cataloging-in-Publication Data

Furstinger, Nancy.
 Say it with music : the story of Irving Berlin / Nancy Furstinger.—
1st ed.
 p. cm. — (Masters of music)
Summary: A biography of the Russian immigrant who came to America as a
boy and became one of the most successful composers of popular songs,
including "White Christmas" and "God Bless America."
Includes bibliographical references (p.) and index.
 ISBN 1-931798-12-5
 1. Berlin, Irving, 1888—Juvenile literature. 2. Composers—United
States—Biography—Juvenile literature. [1. Berlin, Irving, 1888- 2.
Composers. 3. Jews—Biography. 4. Popular music.] I. Title. II. Masters
of music (Greensboro, N.C.)
 ML3930.B446F87 2003
 782.42164'092—dc21

                    2003006039

Printed in the United States of America
First Edition

Modern Music Masters

Irving Berlin

William Grant Still

John Coltrane

George Gershwin

Shinichi Suzuki

Bix Beiderbecke

For my father, Frank Furstinger, whose
play-it-by-ear piano music
and award-winning dancing personify my
favorite Irving Berlin song: "Cheek to Cheek"

Enormous thanks to Mary Ellin Barrett, Irving Berlin's
eldest daughter, for generously sharing her reminiscences
and reviewing the manuscript, and to Bert Fink at The
Rodgers & Hammerstein Organization for
his suggestions and assistance.

Contents

Irving Berlin, 1936.
(Courtesy of the Library of Congress.)

Chapter One

"On the Bum"

No one knows exactly where in Siberia, Russia, Irving Berlin was born. We do know he was the youngest of eight children, and he entered the world on May 11, 1888, as Israel Beilin. This was a turbulent time to be a Jew in Russia. Seven years earlier, Czar Alexander II had been assassinated. Alexander had been more tolerant of his Jewish subjects than many of the other czars. He had allowed the Jews to live in a section of Russia known as the Pale of Settlement. They could not own the land but were left alone to practice their religion. Following his assassination, the new czar, Alexander III, reestablished a policy of anti-Semitism. Cossack soldiers raided and torched Russian-Jewish settlements

Irving Berlin's father, Moses Beilin. *(Courtesy of The Estate of Irving Berlin.)*

in organized attacks, or pogroms. Families were attacked and run off the land. When Israel was five years old, he huddled in a blanket and watched from a hiding place as flames destroyed his home in Temun. This was his only memory of his homeland.

Moses Beilin, Israel's father, eked out a living as a cantor, the official singer during Orthodox Jewish services in synagogues. After his home was burned, there was no reason to stay in Russia; he could not afford to rebuild. Moses decided to relocate his family to the United States. He had friends and relatives who had already made the journey and they wrote to assure him the family would be free to worship without persecution in the United States. He had also heard stories of the fabulous wages and free education that awaited them in the United States.

The summer of 1893, Moses, his wife, Leah, and seven of their children—Ethel, Sarah, Sifre, Benjamin, Rebecca, Chasse, and Israel—traveled across Europe by train, cart, and foot. In Antwerp, Belgium, the Beilins boarded the steamship SS *Rhynland*. They took with them the few possessions saved from the fire—a feather bed and an old brass samovar, or tea urn—and made the eleven-day journey over rough seas.

The Beilins joined other emigrating families below deck of the four-masted steamer. A thousand passengers, paying thirty-five dollars each, were crammed into steerage, so named because of its location near the

Twelve million immigrants passed through Ellis Island in its sixty-two years of operation. *(Courtesy of the Library of Congress.)*

ship's rudder. Passengers from dozens of nations squeezed into the bunks. When the bunkmate above Israel accidentally dropped his pocketknife, the boy received a gash on his forehead. The scar remained a lifelong reminder of his voyage.

On September 23, 1893, the SS *Rhynland* steamed into New York harbor and past the huge Statue of Liberty, which had been presented to the United States by France only seven years earlier. The Beilins disembarked at Ellis Island, the port of entry that had opened in 1890 to process the vast wave of immigrants pouring into the country. The family surname was recorded as Baline, as none of the family spoke English, only Yiddish. After processing, the family was taken by a cousin to their new home in the Lower East Side of Manhattan, where the brick tenements stretched down the bustling streets as far as the eye could see. There were no trees or parks to break the gloom.

In the 1890s, new immigrants from Europe, including Germany, Ireland, Italy, and Russia, made up forty-two percent of New York City's population. More than one-half million of them called the Lower East Side home. A single block could contain three thousand tenants. The Beilins crowded into three rooms in the basement of a tenement on Monroe Street, but soon relocated to a Cherry Street apartment.

It was a drastic change from life in Russia, but Israel,

or Izzy as he was nicknamed, kept an optimistic out-look. "I never felt poverty because I'd never known anything else," he later reminisced. "We had an enor-mous family. Eight or nine in four rooms and in the summer some of us slept on the fire escape or on the roof. I was a boy with poor parents, but let's be realistic about it. I didn't starve. I wasn't cold or hungry. There was always bread and butter and hot tea. I slept better in tenement houses . . . than I do now in a nice bed."

The Statue of Liberty and Ellis Island are both located in New York Harbor. *(Courtesy of the Library of Congress.)*

As a young boy, Irving Berlin sang in the synagogue with his father. *(Courtesy of The Estate of Irving Berlin.)*

Izzy was fascinated by life in America and longed to assimilate into the culture. As the youngest Beilin, he found it easiest to fit into life in his New York neighborhood. Soon he was playing ball and tag on the streets and learned how to shoot marbles and pitch pennies. He skinny-dipped in the East River at the foot of Cherry Street with the other boys as they battled the currents crossing over to Brooklyn.

That first year, Izzy got a glimpse of American holidays. "I was a little Russian-born kid, son of an Orthodox rabbi, living on the Lower East Side of New York City," he recalled. "I did not have a Christmas. I bounded across the street to my friendly neighbors, the O'Haras, and shared their goodies. Not only that, this was my first sight of a Christmas tree. The O'Haras were very poor and later . . . I realized they had to buy one [a tree] with broken branches and small height, but to me that first tree seemed to tower to Heaven."

Izzy's father took jobs as a *shomer*, or kosher poultry inspector; a house painter; and a *mellamud*, or Hebrew teacher. His mother worked as a midwife and assisted women in the tenements when they gave birth. His sisters rolled cigars and his brother sewed shirts in a sweatshop. The Beilins even squeezed in two boarders into their already packed apartment to help with the rent.

Berlin's mother, Leah Beilin, in the early 1900s. *(Courtesy of The Estate of Irving Berlin.)*

Around the age of seven, Izzy enrolled in public school. Teachers thought the boy with the dark dreamy eyes was lazy. "He just dreams and sings to himself," one teacher complained to Izzy's parents. The boy did love to sing. He even sang soprano alongside his father in synagogue.

His teacher may have thought him lazy, but Izzy was certainly industrious after school. He sold newspapers near City Hall. He also sold off pieces of the brass samovar from Russia to a local junk shop. He wanted to buy his mother a rocking chair, which was his idea of a luxurious American item, but there was never enough spare money. By the time he was eight, the second-grader was helping to support his family.

The pennies he earned became more important after Moses died, when Izzy was just thirteen. As a result, he worked even more. Along with a motley crew of news-boys called "newsies," Izzy peddled the *New York Evening Journal,* proudly throwing the pennies he earned each day into his mother's apron. To increase business, he began to sing out the headlines.

One day while he stood on the edge of an East River pier and daydreamed about setting sail on a ship, Izzy was knocked into the river by a crane filling carts of coal. Thrashing in the water among the soggy newspapers, he might have drowned if not for a bystander who jumped in and rescued him. After an ambulance depos-

Newspaper boys selling papers to patrons in a New York saloon.
(Courtesy of the Library of Congress.)

ited him at Gouverneur Hospital, the doctors must have been amazed when they discovered he was still gripping the five pennies he had earned that day.

Although he at first thought he wanted to become a cartoonist, Izzy soon discovered his voice was more valuable than his drawing skills. It came as a surprise, as he remembered later: "Aside from singing in schul [synagogue], I had little musical education. I supposed it was singing with my father that gave me my musical background. It was in my blood."

Izzy preferred the sentimental ballads popular in the 1890s to synagogue chants. Sometimes, while selling papers, he followed the after-work crowds to the rough-and-tumble Bowery saloons where singing waiters served beer for five cents a mug. The more popular songs of the day earned the waiters tips of nickels and dimes flung at their feet. This seemed like a fortune to Izzy compared to the pennies he tossed into his mother's apron. He felt he contributed less than his sisters and he should be earning more money for the family. Rather than be a burden on his mother and siblings, he decided to go "on the bum," the neighborhood slang for leaving his home, family, and schooling behind, and seek his fortune through his voice in the Bowery. He was fourteen years old.

The Bowery, where Izzy hoped to find his fortune, was a gathering place for the downtrodden. It had begun as a trail Native Americans followed during skirmishes with the Dutch and had evolved into an avenue of Lower Manhattan lined with an unsavory assortment of pawnshops, dance halls, boardinghouses, and saloons that served as hangouts for hustlers, sailors from distant ports, streetwalkers, laborers, and lost boys.

Izzy was not attracted to the nightlife waiting within the swinging doors of the saloons. It was the music that beckoned Izzy. Inside, buskers sang the popular songs, such as the bitter "Mansion of Aching Hearts," serving

New York's Bowery in the early 1900s.
(Courtesy of the Library of Congress.)

as a sort of human jukebox. These street singers wandered through the saloons crooning songs in the hopes that customers would pitch their spare change before them onto the sawdust floor. It cost fifteen cents to stay a night in a shabby boardinghouse. An extra dime bought sheets for the bed, and a dinner of chicken fricassee in a local restaurant cost eight cents.

Izzy had to work hard for every cent, but he never lost his optimism. "I always think of my youth in the first decades of the century as the best time of my life," he reminisced later. "My own existence was a struggle from one dollar to the next. But I was finding myself."

In a respite from the Bowery, Izzy briefly sang tenor in the chorus of the musical *The Show Girl*, while it toured the state before opening in New York City. During the show, he served as a song plugger. Izzy pretended to be a spectator captivated by the song "Sammie." He would rise from the balcony and sing the song's chorus spontaneously, or so it seemed.

Pluggers aimed to make a song unforgettable to audience members, who hummed and whistled it as they rushed to buy the sheet music. Printed sheets of popular songs, which sold for several pennies, formed the backbone of the music industry during that time. Instead of being heard on radios or stereos, top tunes reverberated out of parlor pianos across the nation.

After leaving *The Show Girl*, sheet music publisher Harry Von Tilzer hired Izzy to plug songs in Tony Pastor's famed music hall in Union Square. The headline act at Pastor's hall was The Three Keatons, a music and comedy vaudeville act featuring young Buster, who would later become a silent film star. As a song plugger, Izzy earned five dollars a week.

When the Pastor gig was up, Izzy wandered to Chinatown, where he guided a sightless busker called Blind Sol. On successful nights, he made fifty cents. His employment became more stable when Mike Salter hired the teen as a singing waiter in his Pelham Café. During ten-hour shifts, Izzy sang such songs as "Yankee Doodle Dandy" to the accompaniment of the bar pianist. He poured beer as patrons sang along, danced till dawn, and solicited tips to augment his dollar-a-day salary.

In 1904, Chinatown was home to a dangerous opium trade. At the time, opium could legally be purchased over-the-counter at pharmacies. Curious customers went "slumming" at the Pelham Café, hoping to rub elbows with opium addicts and other unsavory characters. Middle-class uptown dwellers thrilled at the idea that the man slumped over a whiskey in the corner could be a criminal, although in reality he was more likely a salesman.

One slumming customer earned Izzy his first printed publicity. Prince Louis of Battenberg sipped beer in the Pelham as Izzy entertained him. Izzy turned down the prince's five-dollar tip and copied Salter's grand gesture of putting the prince's drinks "on the house." Reporters recorded the evening in their newspapers, mentioning Izzy by name.

He next saw his name in print on a piece of sheet music. The pianist and bartender around the corner at Callahan's had composed a song called "My Mariucci Take a Steamboat." Not only was their song published, but it took off. Salter requested a similar tune to bring fame to the Pelham Café. His house pianist, Mike "Nick" Nicholson, teamed up with Izzy, and dashed off a tune.

At nineteen, Izzy sometimes made up parodies of popular songs, so he was a logical choice for lyricist.

"I never wanted to be a songwriter," the reluctant lyricist later said. "All I wanted in those days was a job in which I could earn $25 a week. That was my idea of heaven. But a bartender in another Bowery saloon . . . had written a song . . . and [Salter] sneered at us and asked us why we didn't write something."

The resulting "Marie from Sunny Italy" featured klutzy rhymes like "queen" with "mandolin." Music publisher Joseph W. Stern purchased the song in May of 1907 for the sum of seventy-five cents. Izzy's cut for his first song was thirty-seven cents. His name appeared on the sheet music for "Marie from Sunny Italy" just below the illustration of a gondola. However, the printer had changed his name from Israel Beilin to I. Berlin. "Marie from Sunny Italy" did not thrust I. Berlin into the limelight, but it did encourage him to write several more forgettable songs in the hopes of duplicating the popularity of the songs they imitated.

None of his imitations took off. It was not until he composed an original song that the newly named I. Berlin found his niche. "Dorando" centered around an actual event. An Italian runner by the name of Dorando was disqualified from the 1908 Olympic Games after the crowd shoved him toward the race's finishing line. Berlin dashed off the lyrics for a vaudeville performer who promised him ten dollars but later refused to pay up. Undiscouraged, Izzy plugged the song lyrics to the music publishing firm of Waterson and Snyder. When Henry Waterson asked if Berlin had a tune for the song, he lied, said that he did, and hummed one on the spot for the arranger. Waterson bought the song and Berlin pocketed twenty-five dollars for words and music.

His subsequent ballad, "Sadie Salome (Go Home)," was an even bigger hit and opened the door to steady employment in the music business. He was hired by Waterson and Snyder as an in-house lyricist at a salary of twenty-five dollars a week plus royalties.

Chapter Two

Making the Country Hum

The heartbeat of America's music industry in the early 1900s was on Manhattan's West Twenty-eighth Street. A pedestrian strolling down the street heard a cacophony of sounds: pianos pounding, vocalists singing, composers humming, and lyricists reciting choruses. To the ears of one strolling journalist, West Twenty-eighth Street sounded like the crashing of tin pans. In his newspaper columns, he began referring to the area as "Tin Pan Alley."

Although Thomas Edison had invented sound recording in 1877, sheet music was still how most popular music was introduced to mass audiences. Families gathered in living rooms around the piano to play and sing the latest hit. This created a constant demand for new songs for the evening sing-alongs, a favorite form of middle-class entertainment.

Sheet music was produced following a distinct process. Songwriters collaborated on the lyrics and music, aiming for a blend of memorable yet simple words and melodies. Then an arranger transcribed the song into musical notation for piano and voice. An artist designed the front cover, which was usually an illustration of the theme or a portrait of a singer contracted to perform the song. The cover, music, and lyrics were next sent to the printer. The resulting sheet music was advertised in the music publisher's catalog. Music buyers visited Tin Pan Alley to browse through the catalogs and listen to musicians play the new songs. These buyers sold the sheet music to music shops and department stores all over the nation, whose customers snapped up the latest tunes.

As a way to popularize songs, pluggers were hired to sing them anyplace that attracted a crowd. Some pluggers even carried pianos on horse-drawn carts and traveled to stores, ballparks, saloons, and train platforms to perform. Movie theaters also plugged the songs by flashing the words on the screen as the audience sang along with the house piano player.

Vaudeville singers such as Fanny Brice and Al Jolson also used songs in their shows that toured the country.

Hundreds of vaudeville theaters featured this popular entertainment directed toward mass audiences. The wide assortment of variety acts and singing groups like barbershop quartets created a ceaseless demand for fresh songs.

One successful song could earn a Tin Pan Alley publisher thousands of dollars weekly. The competition was intense between publishers, and the emphasis was on churning out as many songs as possible. This focus on quantity guaranteed that even the best songwriters produced plenty of flops.

Irving Berlin, as he now began to call himself, thrived in the hectic environment at Waterson and Snyder after beginning work there in 1909. He did not know how to read music, much less write it, and he had no musical background or training as a pianist. He began his career writing catchy lyrics to go along with other people's melodies. "Three-fourths of that quality which brings success to popular songs is the phrasing," he explained. "I make a study of it—ease, naturalness, every-day-ness—and it is my first consideration when I start on lyrics. 'Easy to sing, easy to say, easy to remember and applicable to everyday events' is a good rule for a phrase."

One of his earliest songs was "My Wife's Gone to the Country (Hurrah! Hurrah!)." The idea for the piece came from a friend's relief when his wife departed for an extended stay in the country. The happy husband and Berlin collaborated on the words, while his employer, Ted Snyder, composed the melody. The song was a success and sold over three hundred thousand copies of sheet music. Berlin's name was now on the hit list.

After collaborating with Snyder on several more songs, with each man earning a royalty of one cent for every copy of ten-cent sheet music sold, Berlin was featured in an article titled "The Man Who Is 'Making the Country Hum.' " During the interview, Berlin acknowledged his success could vanish overnight. "Song writing all depends on the public. The thing it likes one minute, it tires of the next," he declared. "You must be able to switch your lyre to something else. If not, a new writer will take your place and your star, which rose so suddenly, will set as rapidly as it came up."

Berlin soon proved he was not just talking through his hat in the interview. To improve his chances at sustaining his success, he wanted to learn how to write the entire song—words and music—so he set out to learn how to play the piano. He did so by using the six black and two white keys of F-sharp, which he referred to as "black note keys." "The black keys are right there under your fingers," the novice piano player said, adding, "children who learn to play instinctively always learn on the key of F-sharp."

He would not be confined to the key of F-sharp,

Irving Berlin taught himself to play the piano using the six black and two white keys of F-sharp. *(Courtesy of The Estate of Irving Berlin.)*

however. Tin Pan Alley was full of pianists who did not learn to play their instrument during childhood. They relied on special, transposing pianos, such as the Weser model Berlin bought for one hundred dollars. A transposing piano had a knob to the right of the keyboard (later models had a hidden crank beneath the keyboard). One turn of the wheel shifted the keyboard, and although Berlin continued playing the same keys he did when playing in F-sharp, the notes were in whatever key he had selected. Berlin loved the piano so much he called it his "Buick." He took it wherever he moved, as he literally depended on the piano for his living.

Berlin was soon pounding out melodies to compliment his lyrics. Now that he was the sole writer, Berlin had to learn the proper balance of music and words. "I sacrifice one for the other," he told an interviewer.

> If I have a melody I want to use, I plug away at the lyrics until I make them fit the best parts of my music and vice versa. Nearly all other writers work in teams, one writing the music and the other the words. They are either forced to fit some one's words to their music or some one's music to their words. Latitude—which begets novelty—is denied them, and in consequence both lyrics and melody suffer.

Berlin began to experiment with the newest craze, the lively ragtime music that had its roots in the Mississippi Valley. In the late 1890s, traveling black pianists from this region began to play songs with an incessant ragged, or syncopated, melody line played with the right hand against a standard beat played with the left. African-American Scott Joplin, heralded as the king of ragtime composers, made the music popular among white audiences.

Berlin wrote and performed his first ragtime song, "Oh, That Beautiful Rag," for a 1910 Shubert brothers' show called *Up and Down Broadway*. His next venture into syncopation was "Alexander's Ragtime Band," a piece that would become one of his most famous. Berlin at first released the melody without lyrics, but it flopped when it debuted in a cabaret. Discouraged, Berlin stashed it in his trunk. He later pulled it back out and added lyrics because, as a newly elected Friars' Club member, he was supposed to give a speech. Berlin decided to sing his speech, and the revised "Alexander's Ragtime Band" was the result. It became a hit and soon it could be heard everywhere across America. Before long, it had taken over the music scene in London and Paris. Berlin learned a valuable lesson from this experience. "I wrote it without words as a two-step and it was a dead failure. Six months later, I wrote words to it . . . When the lyrics were added later, it became alive. People sang it and it became a sensation. For music to live, it must be sung."

Scott Joplin composed numerous ragtime pieces, his most famous being the "Maple Leaf Rag." *(Courtesy of Frank Driggs.)*

The song had an irresistible rhythm that made sitting still impossible. Soon a series of colorfully named dances—the turkey trot, bunny hug, fox trot, grizzly bear—sprung up around the tune. These new, wilder dances replaced the polkas and waltzes of the previous generation.

Before it was over, the song that started the new fads, "Alexander's Ragtime Band," sold more than two million copies of sheet music by the end of 1911. The twenty-three-year-old composer was suddenly at the top of the music writing profession. It was exciting, but Berlin was soon worrying about what he could create for an encore.

Berlin's time writing songs for Tin Pan Alley, he acknowledged,

> was very swell for me. I was quite a big shot there. I was an entertainer for about a year and then I went uptown and before long I was writing songs with a drawing account of $25 a week. I'd really had an easy time as a kid, honest. My struggles didn't actually begin until after I'd written 'Alexander's Ragtime Band.' It's been a struggle ever since to keep success going.

Chapter Three

The Hit Maker

By 1912, less than four years after writing "Marie from Sunny Italy," Berlin had earned one hundred thousand dollars in royalties. His ragtime hit, "Alexander's Ragtime Band," continued to sell like "hot-cakes," as Berlin marveled. The song rippled across the world as it was translated into a medley of foreign languages.

Berlin continued to write rags with titles like "Whistling Rag," "The Ragtime Violin," and "Ragtime Mocking Bird," and soon became the dominant writer of rags. When vaudeville star Elsie Janis returned from London to New York, she threw a party that Berlin attended. She entertained her guests by humming bars of a half-dozen of her favorite rags. Berlin, who was meeting her for the first time, proceeded to play each song on a piano. "You certainly have the most phenomenal memory I've ever encountered!" Janis exclaimed. She did not know he had written every one of the songs she had hummed.

"Everybody's Doin' It Now," a catchy commentary on dance crazes such as the turkey trot, became another successful ragtime song for Berlin. Describing this 1911 hit, Berlin said, "I write words and music at the same time. Usually I sit at a piano and pick with one finger. I have in mind some phrase, some line or some idea. For instance the line 'Everybody's Doin' It' was particularly fortunate. It was something universal . . . Everybody is doing something and that was the great catch line of that song. I might call it the spark of the song."

As Berlin's success grew, he became a partner in the music firm where he worked. In January of 1912, Waterson and Snyder officially became Waterson, Berlin & Snyder.

Berlin was no longer sleeping on rented sheets in boarding houses. His new bachelor pad was uptown, far from the Lower East Side, but he continued to create songs that would appeal to residents of his former neighborhood. Years spent on the jammed and bustling streets guaranteed the songwriter would be able to tap into the raw pulse of American music. In his catalog of approximately one hundred songs, many were flavored with foreign dialects: Yiddish, Italian, German, Irish, and

Irving Berlin sitting at a transposing piano with his hand on the lever that allowed him to play in any key. *(Courtesy of The Estate of Irving Berlin.)*

African. They are even more remarkable because they avoided the racial and ethnic stereotypes that were so common in this era. Berlin's intrinsic good nature kept him away from the assumptions of superiority that were taken for granted by many in America. This did not keep his jealous rivals from hinting that Berlin had a black ghostwriter in Harlem who churned out his ragtime hits.

Berlin saw the rumors as confirmation of what he thought most American songwriters were missing. "The reason our American composers have done nothing highly significant is because they won't write American music," he claimed. "They're as ashamed of it as if it were a country relative. So they write imitation European music which doesn't mean anything. Ignorant as I am, from their standpoints, I am doing something they all refuse to do: I'm writing American music."

There was one notable exception to his criticism. Broadway composer George M. Cohan, who wrote such songs as "You're a Grand Old Flag" and "Give My Regards to Broadway," had a distinct American flavor that Berlin admired. Of Cohan, Berlin said, "He was my inspiration, the model, the idol. We all start as imitators of somebody."

Berlin was writing American music and was living the American dream. He took his earnings from "Alexander's Ragtime Band" and surprised his mother with a "country" house in the Bronx, where she could rock back and forth in the rocking chair he had purchased with his first paycheck as a songwriter.

Rich, famous, and dubbed "Berlin the Hit-Maker" by the show business trade magazine *Variety,* the young songwriter was soon in love. Legend has it, when two female singers visited Waterson, Berlin & Snyder requesting a hit tune that might propel them into the limelight, a skirmish over a Berlin song broke out. Berlin settled the fight by giving one woman the song and asking the other, Dorothy Goetz, out on a date.

After a whirlwind courtship, Berlin and Dorothy married on February 2, 1912, and set out for a honeymoon in Cuba. There tragedy struck. Soon after their arrival, the island suffered an outbreak of the infectious typhoid fever. Dorothy contracted the disease. She was ill for weeks, sometimes seeming to rally, but always relapsing, until she died. Five months after his wedding, Berlin was a widower.

He was paralyzed with grief and could not work. "I'm through, finished. If I did have any talent, Ray, it died with Dorothy," Berlin told his brother-in-law. Ray Goetz suggested the songwriter let his emotions work for him. Slowly, Berlin began to follow this advice. He wrote an autobiographical ballad called "When I Lost You." Sheet music sales of the "sob ballad" were over a million copies. The song proved cathartic and helped to ease his grief. Berlin returned to work.

Berlin's next challenge was to write an entire score for a 1914 Broadway musical comedy entitled *Watch Your Step*. Duplicating the work schedule he had kept during his nights as a singing waiter, he stayed up all night until daybreak and composed eighteen original songs. He was under deadline pressure to write enough music to support the production while composing a score to be performed by a twenty-piece orchestra.

Watch Your Step, which was billed as "The First All-Syncopated Musical," became the Broadway hit of the 1914-1915 season and ran for 175 performances. One reviewer wrote, "He [Berlin] has written a score of his mad melodies, nearly all of them of the tickling sort, born to be caught up and whistled at every street corner and warranted to get any roomful a-dancing." Listening to his music performed by an orchestra on opening night at the New Amsterdam Theatre, Berlin later revealed, was the biggest moment of his professional life.

One song stood out. "Play a Simple Melody" interwove a main tune with a syncopated countermelody with both sung simultaneously. The singer of the first verse longs for the sentimental songs like mother sang; the second singer prefers "choppy" ragtime tunes. This marked the first of Berlin's "double songs."

Inspiration for new Broadway songs came from everywhere and could hit anytime. Berlin learned to always be ready. "You write in the morning, you write at night," he once explained. "You write in a taxi, in the bathtub, or in an elevator. And after the song is all finished it may turn out to be very bad, but you sharpen your pencil and try again. A professional songwriter has his mind on his job all the time."

A phrase might pop into his head while he was shaving or strolling. Sometimes the phrase was the song's title and he would then write the verses followed by a repeated chorus that usually echoed the title. Then he got to work on the music. If Berlin was away from his piano, "when the phrase of melody comes to me I work it out mentally. My keyboard is in my mind."

At home Berlin picked out the notes in the key of F-sharp on his Buick, composing the rhythm and melody. Despite his lack of education in music theory, he had an innate mastery of harmony, and his ear selected the right chords instinctively.

Berlin worked throughout the night, chewing gum and chain smoking cigarettes. If the resulting tune pleased his ears, he summoned his musical secretary to write down the score. When he was on a roll, Berlin could compose several songs a week.

They were always simple songs that aimed for the heart. He knew this was the key to his success. "The reason I write simply is that I just wasn't clever when I started. I haven't ever been a Smart Aleck," he told a reporter. "By the time I sharpened the tools of my trade, I found I wrote simple songs because that's how they came out of my head. I didn't try to change anything. A certain emotional something went into the songs and I never tried to analyze it too much. It is often the unselfconscious thing that makes a hit. You can be *too* clever."

Berlin did try music lessons. He lasted two days. "I tried to learn how to read and write music, but I found I was not a student. Besides, in the time I spent taking lessons I could have written a few songs," he said. Formal education, he feared would "ruin" his music, and so he returned to his Buick.

Berlin's tribute to his favorite instrument—"I Love a Piano"—debuted in the 1915 show *Stop! Look! Listen!* While the chorus sang, six pianists played an instrument nearly as long as the Globe Theatre stage was wide. Later the song and its flip side, "The Girl on the Magazine Cover," became the first double-sided number-one hit record.

Berlin was the first to admit not all of his songs were a smashing success. Of his early songwriting career, he confessed, "I wrote more lousy songs than almost anyone else. Some of them may have seemed clever when they were written but they embarrass the hell out of me now. I would be happier if people did not perform them."

Berlin cited some examples in comedian Groucho Marx's book, *The Groucho Letters:*

> Frankly, there are some songs that I would be tempted to pay you not to do . . . "The Friars Parade" is a bad special song I wrote for the Friars Club and you certainly would never have occasion to use that. But why mention individual titles? Let me tell you of my favorite Groucho Marx story the way I tell it: There's a song I wrote during the First World War called "Stay Down Here Where You Belong" of which Groucho knows all the lyrics. Any time he sees me, when I am trying to pose as a pretty good songwriter, he squares off and sings it. I've asked him how much money he will take not to do this but so far he will not be bribed.

Berlin was drafted into the army just a few weeks after becoming a U.S. citizen. *(Courtesy of The Estate of Irving Berlin.)*

Despite his immense success, Berlin remained self-critical. When a young admirer gushed, "Oh, Mr. Berlin, I guess there's no one who has written as many hits as you have," he retorted, "I know there's no one who has written so many failures."

On February 26, 1918, Irving Berlin passed his proudest personal milestone. On that day, he took the oath of allegiance and became a citizen of the United States. Nearly thirty years old, the new American civilian received a letter from President Woodrow Wilson a few weeks later. He at first thought it was a congratulation from the president. It was his draft notice. Irving Berlin was going to be a solider in the U.S. Army.

President Wilson had asked Congress for a declaration of war against Germany in April 1917. The war began in 1914, but the United States refused to become part of it for the first years. Now the United States was finally entering World War I. Berlin received orders to report to Camp Upton in Yaphank, New York, on Long Island. News of his induction spurred tabloid headlines screaming "Army Takes Berlin!" He went from being a famous songwriter to a lowly thirty-dollar-a-week private—forced to rise at five o'clock in the morning.

For a night owl like Private Berlin, who never went to bed earlier than 2 A.M., this was the worst part about being a soldier. He hated the morning bugle call. "There were a lot of things about army life I didn't like, and the thing I didn't like most of all was reveille. I hated it," Berlin complained. "I hated it so much I used to lie awake nights thinking about how much I hated it."

Determined to be a good soldier, Berlin made himself get up when the bugle blew. He even pretended he enjoyed getting up early. "The other soldiers thought I was a little too eager about it, and they hated me. That's why I finally wrote a song about it."

"Oh! How I Hate to Get Up in the Morning" not only restored Berlin's reputation among his fellow soldiers, it became a huge wartime hit.

Soon promoted to sergeant, Berlin came up with a way to escape reveille. When Major General J. Franklin Bell suggested Sergeant Berlin stage a show to raise thirty-five thousand dollars to build a visitors' center at Camp Upton, Berlin agreed, but he informed the general he was accustomed to working through the night. He was granted permission to skip reveille and concentrate on the show.

The red, white, and blue revue, *Yip, Yip, Yaphank,* combined songs with comedy sketches in a professionally staged production. Three hundred and fifty soldiers, known as "doughboys," served up "A Military Musical 'Mess' Cooked Up by the Boys of Camp Upton," as the revue was dubbed. On stage at the Century Theatre in Manhattan, khaki-clad soldiers boxed, danced, juggled, drilled, and of course, sang. Since no female soldiers occupied Camp Upton, cross-dressing males mimicked chorus lines. Sergeant Berlin sang his solo, "Oh! How I Hate to Get Up in the Morning."

One Berlin song did not make the final cut. The songwriter wanted to salute his adopted country with a patriotic tune. When Berlin played his new song, "God Bless America," for Harry Ruby, his musical secretary, Ruby had doubts. "See, there were so many patriotic songs coming out everywhere at that time," Ruby remembered. "It was 1918, and every songwriter was pouring them out. He'd already written several patriotic numbers for the show, and when he brought in 'God Bless America,' I took it down for him, and I said, 'Geez, *another* one?' And I guess Irving took me seriously. He put it away."

Berlin admitted, "It seemed a little like painting the lily having soldiers sing it." He stored the song in his trusty trunk.

Yip, Yip, Yaphank earned eighty-three thousand dollars during its thirty-two performances. General Bell, who delivered a speech at the premier, praised Berlin. "I have heard that Berlin is among the foremost songwriters of the world, and now I believe it," he said. "Berlin is as good a soldier as he is a songwriter, and as popular in Camp Upton as he is on Broadway."

A few months later the war was over and Irving Berlin was back in New York.

Chapter Four

New Music for New Action

A new battle had exploded on the home front towards the end of World War I, this time within the music industry. Sheet music sales plummeted as people raced to purchase records to listen to on their Victrolas, or "talking machines." One-sided discs, costing around a dollar, delivered two to three minutes of music. Tin Pan Alley went from a hit factory to old news seemingly over night.

Berlin proved his stamina by weathering the transition. After scoring *The Ziegfeld Follies of 1919,* an extravagant Broadway production running for 171 performances, the songwriter also boasted a successful record. "You'd Be Surprised," sung by Eddie Cantor in the *Follies* and on the recording, racked up sales of eight hundred thousand records, equaling its sheet-music sales.

To remain popular, Berlin stopped penning ragtime tunes. Now he composed elegant melodies matched with tasteful lyrics—songs that would fulfill any plugger's dream by remaining memorable long after being heard. As he wrote in the *Follies* sophisticated theme song, "A Pretty Girl Is Like a Melody":

> Most every year we're haunted
> By some little popular tune;
> Then someone writes another—
> The old one's forgotten soon.

His unforgettable songs were soon showcased in an unusual venture. It began with an offhand comment that Berlin made to Sam Harris, a Broadway producer. The songwriter suggested Harris consider building a theater devoted to musical comedy. Harris took Berlin up on his offer, and the men formed a partnership.

After selecting a site on West Forty-fifth Street in Manhattan's theater district, the partners oversaw construction of the theater they would name the Music Box. With a lavish, four-column exterior and elegant chandeliers gracing the interior, the Music Box's budget quickly swelled to an astronomical $947,000.

Building the new theater put pressure on Berlin.

Despite declining to have his name attached to the Music Box—"too much Berlin," he objected—he recognized it served a unique function as the only theater built to showcase a single composer. Berlin's revues needed to sell tickets, and plenty of them.

Luckily, he worked best under pressure. "I can't get to work until my partners tell me that sales are falling, that the rent is increasing, that salaries are going up—all because I'm not on the job. Then I sweat blood. Absolutely, I sweat blood between 3 and 6 many mornings and when the drops that fall off my forehead hit the paper, they're notes," Berlin said.

The notes fell into place for the *Music Box Revue of 1921,* which opened on September 22. The theater's theme song, "Say It with Music," was introduced in the score. A smashing success, the revue earned a profit of nine thousand dollars a week, enough to let the show go on for forty-one weeks with 440 performances.

The jazzy "Pack Up Your Sins (and Go to the Devil)," a double song in the *Revue of 1922*, demonstrated Berlin's ability to keep up with trends. On the cusp of the Jazz Age, the composer explained the transition in musical tastes:

> It was the age of the automobile. The speed and snap of American jazz music is influenced by the automobile's popularity. Wagner, Beethoven, Mendelssohn, Liszt. All the masters of music knew

the value of movement. All the old rhythm is gone and in its place is heard the hum of an engine, the whirr of wheels, the explosion of an exhaust. The leisurely songs that men hummed to the clatter of horse's hoofs do not fit into this new rhythm. The new age demands new music for new action.

The Jazz Age, also known as the Roaring Twenties, followed the successful outcome of World War I. It was a prosperous decade that saw the introduction of modern conveniences and an increase in leisure time. New audiences listened to music on new technology. Not only were records gaining in popularity, but radios appeared on the scene. Millions of American households purchased the boxes on the installment plan. The new entertainment system, along with the Victrola, began to replace the parlor piano and its accompanying sheet music. Now songs could become overnight successes.

Confidence in his past and future hits encouraged the composer to establish his own company in 1919. Irving Berlin, Inc. published his songs as well as those of other composers. That same year, an "Irving Berlin Week" took place across America, with his songs played in theaters, dance halls, and nightclubs.

Although Berlin suffered great artistic pains while creating his songs, he always took care of the business side of songwriting. Irving Berlin, Inc. reflected that philosophy. "Usually, writing songs is a matter of having to pay bills and sitting down to make the money to pay them with," he said. Now he would have more of the profits to help pay his bills.

Some of Berlin's new songs were in the "sob ballad" style, including "What'll I Do?" and "All Alone." They were not, he insisted, autobiographical. "It has always been assumed that whenever I've written a ballad I've been through some heartbreaking experience. But the real reason is that the public would rather buy tears than smiles—and right now they happen to want sob ballads."

The songwriter spent more time "all alone feeling blue" than he cared to admit, though. Although Berlin palled around with members of the Round Table—a group of playwrights, journalists, artists, and actors who lunched at the Algonquin Hotel—he had remained romantically unattached since the death of his first wife. That changed when he attended a dinner party in May of 1924 and met Ellin Mackay. The attraction was instant and mutual, but there were problems. Ellin's background could not have been more different than Berlin's. Her grandfather had made his fortune with the Comstock Lode silver mines and her father headed a telegraph and cable corporation. Wealthy and Roman Catholic, the Mackays lived in a palatial Long Island mansion named Harbor Hill.

During dinner, Ellin praised Berlin's new song, which she mistakenly called "What Shall I Do?" The songwriter admitted, "With grammar, I can always use a little help." Later the couple visited a cabaret where Berlin once worked as a singing waiter. Back at his studio piano, he played and sang a medley of his songs for her "in a high, wispy, always true voice." For her part, Ellin could not carry a tune, admitting that she was tone deaf.

When the romance deepened, the couple encountered the roadblock of Ellin's father. Clarence Mackay was a lover of classical music who viewed Broadway and show business with suspicion. The cleft between Berlin and Ellin's backgrounds was insurmountable, Mackay believed, which made the success of a marriage between them unfeasible.

The headstrong Ellin was not to be dissuaded. The next year, writing in the *New Yorker,* she stated, "Modern girls are conscious of their identity and they marry whom they choose, satisfied to satisfy themselves."

Determined to thwart the relationship, Mr. Mackay took Ellin abroad for a six-month European tour. The couple continued to communicate, albeit, clandestinely. In one letter, Berlin confided, "I really am delighted with a good deal of my stuff, but I have lived with it so long and gone over the numbers so often that they have become stale. Then again, as I told you so many times, the thrill of the Music Box has gone and now it has

The Marx Brothers, from top to bottom, Chico, Harpo, Groucho, and Zeppo. *(Courtesy of the Library of Congress.)*

become a job that I love most when it's finished."

He had written the *Music Box Revue of 1921, 1922, 1923,* and *1924* while sequestered in an Atlantic City hotel. "The only breath of salt air I got for weeks at a time was when I leaned out of a window and flew a kite," he said.

The pressure of composing these annual revues, which were declining in popularity on Broadway, drove Berlin to eventually rent out the Music Box to other producers. This freed him to tackle the score for *The Cocoanuts,* a musical comedy starring the Marx Brothers. The four brothers reprised the same shtick that had made them a popular vaudeville act for fifteen years.

Their unpredictable jests and spontaneous improvising, which was the source of their humor, created countless difficulties for Berlin and for playwright George S. Kaufman, whose script was changed so much that he was overheard quipping, "I think I just heard one of my own lines." The brothers constantly ad-libbed and added new comedy bits, forcing Berlin to cut his songs. Berlin hinted at one point that soon they would "have a musical without music."

One song that didn't make *The Cocoanuts* cut— "Always"—became famous anyway when the composer gave it to his new bride as a wedding present. On January 4, 1926, Berlin and Ellin eloped. After rushing to the Municipal Building for the ceremony, they discovered neither one had the two-dollar fee for the marriage license. After Berlin's office manager paid up, a crowd of reporters trailed the newlyweds as they tried to slip away on their honeymoon.

Ellin's father, furious about the marriage, disinherited her. The new Ellin Berlin gave up ten million dollars for love, although she maintained her personal trust fund. Other high society friends of the Mackays also snubbed Ellin for marrying a man connected with the theater and who was also Jewish. To escape the controversy, the Berlins honeymooned abroad, and later resided in London and Paris, to wait for the storm to blow over. When they returned to the West Forty-sixth

Street building Berlin called home, they soon welcomed their first child, a daughter they named Mary Ellin. The sentimental father harkened back to his own childhood roots and composed "Russian Lullaby" to sooth the baby to sleep.

Another song expressing the optimism that he received from his new wife and child, "Blue Skies," became the biggest hit of 1927 when Al Jolson sang it in

The newly-wed Berlins in Atlantic City.
(Courtesy of The Estate of Irving Berlin.)

The Jazz Singer. This historic movie was the first fea-
ture-length "talkie" film, combining spoken dialogue
and musical performances to advance the dramatic action. A new era had begun as silent films faded from the
screen. The technology had advanced again, and once
again Irving Berlin would be a part of the change.

Chapter Five

A Crack of Insecurity

As the Roaring Twenties neared a close, Berlin's blue skies turned dark. Ellin gave birth to a son they named Irving on December 1, 1928. The baby died a few weeks later, on Christmas morning.

A gloom descended upon the entire country the following year. On a day now known as Black Thursday, October 24, 1929, the prices on the New York Stock Exchange crashed. This was the end of the boom twenties and the beginning of the Great Depression. Over the next few years, banks and businesses shut their doors all over the country. Thousands of Americans lost life savings and lines at the free soup kitchens snaked around blocks. Millionaires became paupers overnight and once hard-working husbands and fathers left their families and struck out on their own, as they were not earning any money and their absence would mean one less mouth to feed.

Berlin himself lost a fortune—twenty years of savings and every penny he had invested in the stock market, a figure estimated at five million dollars, equivalent in today's market to about fifty million dollars. They were lucky that Ellin's trust fund money, cautiously invested, had not vanished. "Luckily I had a rich wife," Berlin later quipped.

The Great Depression made a wide crack in the confidence and security of Americans. Berlin admitted, "I was scared. I had had all the money I wanted for the rest of my life. Then all of a sudden I didn't . . . I found I'd have to go back to work, and I wasn't sure I could make the grade. I used to write a song and take it for granted that it was all right. Now I found I was very critical of myself and would ask opinions of all sorts of people before putting a number out."

After years of dashing off hits, Berlin "developed the damnedest feeling of inferiority" when four of the five songs he wrote for the 1930 film *Reaching for the Moon* were cut. "Musicals were the rage out there" in Hollywood "and all of a sudden they weren't," the songwriter lamented. His insecure feelings mirrored the nation's. Would his future endeavors measure up?

Incapacitated by his dry spell, Berlin's inferiority complex deepened when he thought of the new, younger competition. For example, George Gershwin was clearly hitched to a rising star. Gershwin had been a Tin Pan Alley piano player who Berlin once asked to write down one of his songs. Berlin could hear Gershwin was a splendid pianist. He commented, "George took it down, and he played it so that I just didn't recognize it, it was so beautiful." He refused to hire Gershwin as an arranger. Instead, he advised him to "Stick to your own songs, kid, you're too good to be arranging some other songwriter's music." In 1931, Gershwin had a hit musical, *Of Thee I Sing,* that was drawing crowds to Berlin's Music Box.

Berlin slowly emerged from his drought and wrote a Broadway show of his own called *Face the Music.* Premiered in 1932, it reflected the turbulent times by opening with a group of socialites dining in an automat and singing "Let's Have Another Cup of Coffee." This later became the theme song of Horn & Hardart Automats, where a handful of nickels inserted into chrome and glass compartments could purchase an entire meal.

One duet from *Face the Music,* "I Don't Wanna Be Married (I Just Wanna Be Friends)" was considered too scandalous to publish because its lyrics suggested a woman would prefer to remain single, even after having a child.

Another song, "I Say It's Spinach," was based on a 1927 *New Yorker* magazine cartoon. The caption, "I say it's spinach and the hell with it," written by editor E.B. White, was a cartoon child's response when his mother urged him to eat his broccoli. It had since become a carefree slogan. Although *Face the Music* was not a big hit due to declining Broadway ticket sales during the Depression, the show reestablished Berlin's reputation as a major American popular composer.

The composer's notoriety for picking out songs on the piano with one finger was quashed around this time, when Berlin invited reporters to a recital. The rumor vanished after a journalist wrote, "It was a simple demonstration, but it did take in eight fingers and two thumbs."

Ironically, the songwriter scored a big hit on radio in 1932 when Rudy Vallee sang his "Say It Isn't So." Berlin had been slow to warm to radio. This was due, in part, because he saw its "free music" as an economic threat. He also disliked it for more aesthetic reasons: "We have become a world of listeners, rather than singers. Our songs don't live anymore. They fail to become part of us. Radio has mechanized them all."

Berlin tackled another musical in 1933. *As Thousands Cheer* featured songs and skits that parodied a daily newspaper—headlines, politics, business, gossip, weather, even comic strips—and was a smashing success. It opened with the comical number "Man Bites Dog," and spotlighted songs that have become classics, such as the sizzling "Heat Wave" and the tragic "Supper Time." The last song was performed by African-American star Ethel Waters for a scene titled "Unknown Negro Lynched by Frenzied Mob." As the wife of the victim, Waters' character wonders how to tell her children that their father will not be coming home for supper. The woman cries out "Lord!" prompting one critic to write, "Nowhere else in American song have I heard a single note and a single word combined so shatteringly."

The most successful song in the show demonstrated

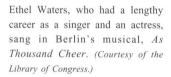

Ethel Waters, who had a lengthy career as a singer and an actress, sang in Berlin's musical, *As Thousand Cheer*. *(Courtesy of the Library of Congress.)*

Berlin's penchant for borrowing from old work. "Easter Parade" recast the melody of a 1917 flop, "Smile and Show Your Dimple," with new lyrics. "A song is like a marriage," Berlin explained. "It takes a perfect blending of the two mates, the music and the words, to make a perfect match. In the case of 'Easter Parade' it took a divorce and a second marriage to bring about the happiest of unions."

The following year, Berlin embarked on a new adventure when he traded in the bright lights of Broadway for Hollywood. The movie industry had begun luring Broadway and Tin Pan Alley songsters west to work on movie musical scores. This launched what most consider to be a golden age of movie musicals, a period that lasted from around 1930 through 1955. Most of the great American popular composers switched back and forth between the stage and film during these years. Berlin was no exception.

Always an astute businessman, Berlin insisted RKO Pictures give him ten percent of gross profits of any film he worked on in exchange for his accepting a smaller salary. Berlin's first film for the studio was the 1935 Fred Astaire and Ginger Rodgers musical comedy *Top Hat*. His score featured five songs that advanced the lighthearted boy-meets-girl plot. The enchanting seventy-two-bar "Cheek to Cheek," a masterpiece of the movie musical that Berlin dashed off in a single day, contained this romantic rhapsody:

Heaven,
I'm in heaven,
And my heart beats so
That I can hardly speak,
And I seem to find
The happiness I seek
When we're out together dancing
Cheek to cheek.

One of movies finest film scores, *Top Hat* earned its composer financial and critical acclaim. All five songs made musical history when they aired together on "Your Hit Parade," a Saturday night program spotlighting the

Irving Berlin plays the piano for Fred Astaire and Ginger Rogers, who starred together in Berlin's *Top Hat. (Courtesy of The Estate of Irving Berlin.)*

week's fifteen most popular tunes. "Cheek to Cheek" was in first place. No one had ever approached such a record. The film earned more than three million dollars, from which Berlin received a ten-percent cut.

In 1936, *Follow the Fleet* again paired Astaire and Rodgers. In this romance, the dancing duo rescues each other from shipboard suicide to the tune of "Let's Face the Music and Dance." It was another success.

Another all-American musical, this time for Twentieth-Century Fox and released in 1938, took its title from Berlin's 1911 hit "Alexander's Ragtime Band." A combination of twenty-six old and three new songs made up most of the plot that followed a band leader named Alexander, who advances from Broadway to Camp Upton to the Music Box and finally to Carnegie Hall.

Berlin insisted *Alexander's Ragtime Band* was not his own musical biography, although it was the first film to credit a songwriter's name above the title. Berlin contended the progression of songs traced a twenty-seven-year period in American popular music. Music hall dance crazes of the 1910s, patriotic WWI songs, 1920s sob ballads, and radio crooners of the 1930s, were all were woven into the musical. It was a musical history of the first decades of twentieth century America. The songs earned an Academy Award for best scoring of a musical.

Chapter Six

God Bless America

In the last years of the 1930s, America and Europe were faced with the ominous rise in power of Adolph Hitler and Nazi Germany. Despite the best efforts of the world's diplomats, Hitler began expanding his power in 1938 by absorbing Austria and Czechoslovakia into his Third Reich. It became clear to many that a new European war was on the horizon. Berlin sensed it was time for a patriotic song to help rally American morale. He also wanted to reaffirm his love for the country that had given him and his family a home and opportunity.

When he set to work on the song, though, he found it tough going. Patriotism was harder to put to music than love and longing. "I worked for a while on a song called 'Thanks, America' but didn't like it. I tried again with a song called 'Let's Talk About Liberty,' but I didn't get very far with that. I found it was too much like making a speech to music," he said.

Eventually, he remembered a song he had written years before. He found "God Bless America" in the trunk where he had put it after jettisoning it from *Yip, Yip, Yaphank* almost twenty-one years earlier. The title of the song had been inspired by Berlin's mother, who, despite struggling to survive in the tenements, would proudly declare, "God bless America."

Berlin modernized the lyrics from the original version, but kept the term "America" rather than switching to the more precise "United States" because he knew it would arouse more patriotism in the listener. He also changed the original line reading, "Make her victorious on land and foam" to "From the mountains to the prairies to the oceans white with foam.'"

Writing a great peace song was "hard to do, because you have trouble dramatizing peace . . . Yet music is so important. It changes thinking, it influences everybody, whether they know it or not."

Simple, yet strong, the song went out over the airwaves on Armistice Day of 1938 when popular singer Kate Smith belted out "God Bless America" on her CBS radio show. She introduced it as "one of the most beautiful compositions ever written, a song that will never die." In schools, churches, theaters, and ballparks across the country, "God Bless America" caught on like wild-fire. It even boosted the long dormant sale of sheet music. There was talk of Berlin's new hit replacing "The Star-Spangled Banner" as the national anthem, although Berlin was opposed to this.

Berlin thought his song "caught on because it happens to have a universal appeal." His patriotic song was written so that everyone could sing it. "All that I hope for 'God Bless America,' " Berlin said, "is that it will continue to be popular, especially in these days when so many people feel a need for some vocal expression of their patriotism." Both the Democratic and Republican parties shared his patriotic sentiments, and each adopted "God Bless America" as their official song during the 1940 presidential campaign.

The songwriter claimed "God Bless America" meant more to him than any other song. It was a proclamation of his gratitude to his adopted country. Berlin donated all the royalties he earned from it to the Girl Scouts and Boy Scouts of America. Over the decades, the scouts have reaped millions from Berlin's generosity.

Over the Christmas holidays of 1940, Berlin purchased a home and fifty acres in the Catskill Mountain town of Lew Beach. He wanted a place outside of the city where he could enjoy the quiet. His family, which now included daughters Mary Ellin, Linda Louise, and Elizabeth Irving, could relax while Berlin pursued his

When this picture was taken in 1942, Irving and Ellin Berlin had been married sixteen years and had three daughters. *(Courtesy of The Estate of Irving Berlin.)*

new passion for trout fishing on a tributary of the Beaverkill River. "For the first time in my life I'm interested in something besides my work," he said. "I hope it lasts."

It didn't. He was soon back behind his Buick composing more patriotic songs. As America grew closer to entering World War II, he turned out "When That Man Is Dead and Gone" about Hitler, whom he called "Satan with a small moustache." "Angels of Mercy" became the American Red Cross anthem, and "The President's

Birthday Ball" spurred the March of Dimes campaign. "Any Bonds Today?" helped the Treasury Department sell defense bonds. "I Paid My Income Tax Today" was a nod to the Internal Revenue Service.

In 1940, back on Broadway after a seven-year absence, Berlin tackled a new musical comedy entitled *Louisiana Purchase.* It included songs such as "Fools Fall in Love." "It's a Lovely Day Tomorrow" harmonized with the storyline of a campaigning senator in the South.

Although Berlin's songs could be heard live, they were not available on the air. Broadcasters had refused to sign a new contract with the American Society of Composers, Authors, and Publishers (ASCAP). The dispute was over fees for playing the records on the radio, and when the contract negotiation broke down, it meant no song under copyright could be played on radio.

Berlin was a co-founder of ASCAP, which had been created in 1914 to protect songwriter's copyrights by systemizing how royalties were collected and distributed. When the boycott began, Berlin said, "The public has been getting the cream of the bottle, after the first of the year they will be getting skimmed milk." The public had no choice but to listen to old, out of copyright songs as the boycott continued. In the meantime, Berlin got busy with his next project. He had a long-term goal of producing a song for each American holiday. He had already penned "Easter Parade," (Easter); "Be Careful, It's My Heart," (Valentine's Day); "Let's Say It with Firecrackers," (Independence Day); "Plenty to Be Thankful For," (Thanksgiving); and "Let's Start the New Year Right" (New Year).

The plot of the 1942 film musical *Holiday Inn* revolved around Christmas. When Berlin began work, the lyrics and music came to him in a quicksilver flash of inspiration. As Berlin later described it:

> We working composers all too often, in the interests of expediency, sharpen our pencils, get out that square sheet of paper and become too slick. Those forced efforts are 'square' songs. But sometimes a song is a natural. We may start it to order for a specific scene or show, but our subconscious beings go to work and the song is just there. This is what I call a 'round' song.

His "round" song, "White Christmas," contained simple, sentimental lyrics:

> I'm dreaming of a white Christmas
> Just like the ones I used to know,
> Where the treetops glisten
> And children listen
> To hear sleigh bells in the snow.

Berlin might have been remembering the first Christmas he had celebrated with the O'Haras and their lopsided tree on the Lower East Side. This quality of seeming to come from deep inside the composer is what gives "White Christmas" its continuing power. He was so anxious over the song's show-stopping ability, he hid behind the sound screens when Bing Crosby recorded "White Christmas" for *Holiday Inn.* Crosby confidently told him to not worry about his newest creation. It was a sure winner.

Crosby was right. When *Holiday Inn* premiered in 1942, the United States had recently entered World War II and "White Christmas," with its imagery of gathered family and friends in a greeting card setting, appealed to the soldiers overseas and the families left behind.

"It came out at a time when we were at war and it became a peace song in wartime—a meaning I had never intended," Berlin said. "It started off just as a song for a lazy person who only liked working on the holidays. But it was nostalgic to a lot of boys who weren't home for Christmas. Some of them were in the South Pacific where there were no 'White Christmases.'"

Berlin also did not plan for "White Christmas" to become the bestselling Christmas song of all time— although he boasted it was the best song anybody ever wrote about the holiday. It was his most popular song and has sold over 125 million recordings (with Crosby's version alone accounting for thirty-one million copies) and who knows how many copies of sheet music. When the Oscars were awarded, "White Christmas" won the

Irving Berlin put on his World War I uniform to sing "Oh, How I Hate to Get Up in the Morning" in *This Is the Army. (Courtesy of The Estate of Irving Berlin.)*

Academy Award for Best Original Song of 1942. Ironically, Berlin always preferred to spend his Christmases in sunny places.

After winning the Oscar, Berlin wrote a modest couplet: "There goes Time with your last year's prize, Whittling it down to its proper size."

After the United States entered World War II in December of 1941, Berlin signed up to put on a show starring soldiers. This time around, the army agreed to release more than three hundred soldiers for *This Is the Army*. All box office receipts along with sheet music and record royalties were pledged to the Army Emergency Relief Fund.

To get into the spirit, Berlin and company rehearsed at Camp Upton, where nearly a quarter of a century before he composed *Yip, Yip, Yaphank*. Mirroring his earlier revue, *This Is the Army* also featured dancers, jugglers, comedians, female impersonators, and of course, singers—including Berlin in his old WWI uniform singing "Oh, How I Hate to Get Up in the Morning." What *This Is the Army* did not contain were blackface routines. Rather than using white soldiers in blackface, Berlin signed up black performers.

Service men and women involved in producing *This Is the Army* became the only integrated armed forces unit serving during World War II. When the show went on tour, Berlin said:

Berlin met back stage with Eleanor Roosevelt, who enjoyed *This Is the Army* so much she attended several performances. *(Courtesy of The Estate of Irving Berlin.)*

We always insisted that the black guys stay with us. And if a place wouldn't take us, all three hundred of us would go where the black guys could go. We wouldn't play in a segregated theater—and that's that. We were invited to a party on occasion, and a couple of times, they didn't include the black guys. We said, 'We're sorry, we're not coming. Forget it.'

On July 4, 1942, *This Is the Army* debuted on Broadway, where it raised fifty thousand dollars. The biggest laugh from the show came from one private's wisecrack to his sergeant, "Go ahead, break me. Make me a civilian." It went on to become a WWII slogan. Of *This Is the Army,* Berlin said, "It's the biggest emotional experience of my life. I don't think I've ever had a moment to match this."

The moment, though, would extend longer than he had anticipated. At the urging of Eleanor Roosevelt, the show traveled to Washington, D.C. so that President Franklin D. Roosevelt could attend. From there, *This Is the Army* journeyed on a whirlwind national tour to major cities, earning another two million dollars.

Warner Brothers decided to make a movie version in 1943 that starred future President Ronald Reagan, then a lieutenant and contract player for the studio. Berlin sang his WWI hit, "Oh, How I Hate to Get Up in the Morning" on film. His trembling voice prompted one electrician to scoff, "If the guy who wrote this song could hear the way this guy is singing it, he'd turn over in his grave." Despite the quality of Berlin's voice, the film raised more than $9.5 million for the army and won an Academy Award for best score.

This Is the Army even traveled across the Atlantic to entertain audiences overseas, including military personnel in all major combat areas. During the British leg of the tour, Berlin met General Dwight D. Eisenhower when he came backstage after the show. He also met

Princess Elizabeth and British Prime Minister Winston S. Churchill. In Rome, he was granted an audience with Pope Pius XII. The show continued even after Germany surrendered. The war with Japan ended on September 2, 1945. The following month, *This Is the Army* concluded its run with a finale performance in Hawaii.

In October, Berlin accepted the Medal of Merit from President Harry S. Truman. The official citation read: "He has set a high standard of devotion to his country and has won for himself the thanks and appreciation of the United States Army for highly meritorious service." *This Is the Army*, along with "God Bless America," secured Berlin's status as the greatest American composer of patriotic songs.

Chapter Seven

Show Business

Irving Berlin was not the first choice to write the score for a new Broadway show called *Annie Get Your Gun*, about Annie Oakley, the female sharpshooter who became famous in Buffalo Bill's Famous Wild West Show. The team of Richard Rodgers and Oscar Hammerstein II were going to produce the show and had originally commissioned Jerome Kern. A celebrated composer in his own right, Kern once said: "Irving Berlin has no place in American music: he *is* American music. Emotionally, he honestly absorbs the vibrations emanating from the people, manners and life of his time and, in turn, gives these impressions back to the world—simplified, clarified and glorified."

Irving Berlin wrote the score of *Annie Get Your Gun* for composer Richard Rodgers (*left*) and lyricist Oscar Hammerstein II (*right*). *(Courtesy of The Estate of Irving Berlin.)*

Tragically, Kern died suddenly from a cerebral hemorrhage before he could work on the score. Rodgers and Hammerstein asked Berlin to replace him. At first, Berlin had doubts he could pull it off. He was not a young man any longer. "At my age, 'over twenty-one,' this seems like a second helping. Every time I start with a show I wonder if this time I'll reach for it and find it isn't there," he confided.

The project did have its allure, though. He always preferred the immediacy of Broadway to working in the movies. "All that time [between writing songs for film and the film being released] the songs are hidden away and you have no way of knowing whether the songs will be accepted or rejected," Berlin said.

When he began working on the songs for *Annie Get Your Gun*, Berlin retreated to Atlantic City. "There was only one act at that time—a first draft called *Annie Oakley*. I read it and liked it very much but didn't think it was quite up my alley." He reluctantly read the first act again and began writing songs.

He may have had doubts when he began work, but the music he produced proved to everyone, except maybe

(*From left to right*) Composers John Philip Sousa, Harry B. Smith, Jerome Kern, Irving Berlin, and George W. Meyer. *(Courtesy of the Library of Congress.)*

the self-critical composer, that he still had what it took to compose for the stage. The unforgettable tune "You Can't Get a Man with a Gun" accentuated the rivalry between sharpshooter Annie Oakley and Frank Butler, a co-star of Buffalo Bill's Wild West Show. "Doin' What Comes Natur'lly" came after Berlin decided he would have to drop out of the show because he could not write "hillbilly" lyrics. Hammerstein refused to accept his resignation and advised, "All you have to do is drop the G's," and Berlin went back to work. Later, when Rodgers asked for a "challenge song" between Annie and Frank, Berlin dashed off "Anything You Can Do" during a fifteen-minute taxi ride.

One of the songs for *Annie Get Your Gun* vanished from the score when Berlin mistakenly believed Rodgers and Hammerstein did not appreciate it. Reacting to the perceived criticism, he stashed the song in his trunk. Later, it was put back in the script, and when sung by Ethel Merman, who played Annie, "There's No Business Like Show Business" became the unofficial anthem of Broadway.

When *Annie Get Your Gun* opened in May of 1946, it was a smash hit. It ran for 1,147 performances. Berlin's score, now considered by many to be his masterpiece, was one of the biggest hits in the history of Broadway musicals. It produced a record nine hit songs. "There's No Business Like Show Business," the tune that almost vanished from the show, came to epitomize Berlin's success as a songwriter.

"I've always thought of myself as a songwriter," he said. "What else would I want to be? I'm a songwriter, like dozens and dozens of others, and so long as I'm able, whether the songs are good or bad, I'll continue to write them, because song writing is not alone a business or a hobby with me. It's everything."

Even the occasional negative criticism could not dampen his dedication to the craft of song writing. After an envious songwriter labeled *Annie Get Your Gun* "old fashioned," Berlin responded to his rival, "Yeah, a good old-fashioned smash." And when he read critic Brooks Atkinson's review panning *Annie*'s songs as "undistinguished," Berlin answered with a rhetorical question. "Aren't we lucky that the critics only *write about* the music and don't try to *write it* themselves?"

In October 1946, Berlin was awarded the Roosevelt Medal. The other recipients were two generals, Dwight D. Eisenhower and Douglas MacArthur. Berlin was introduced as "an American by choice—a patriot who shares with his countrymen his gifts, his time, his energy and his earnings—a singer whose songs warm the hearts of the 140 million Americans."

Attorney General Tom C. Clark invited Berlin to Washington, D.C. to discuss an idea he had for a commemorative exhibit on American life. The exhibit would

travel across the U.S. on a train. "I got terribly excited
about his idea," Berlin recalled. "After that first meeting, his idea kept growing and . . . I started thinking
about a song called 'The Freedom Train.' "

With his characteristic enthusiasm, Berlin dashed
off the song during the weekend, and the following
week Bing Crosby and the Andrew Sisters recorded it.
"The Freedom Train" debuted live in Philadelphia on
September 17, 1947, to coincide with the run of the
actual train.

In response to a high-school student's letter about
"The Freedom Train," Berlin wrote:

> I can only say that as an immigrant who came to this
> country over fifty years ago, I have had a front row
> seat in watching freedom at work. Everything I have
> and everything I am, I owe to this country, which is the
> main reason why I thought the Freedom Train was
> important enough to write a song about. I'm glad you
> like the song and I hope it becomes worthy of the great
> subject that inspired it.

Berlin's contagious songs continued to affect American audiences. Two MGM musical films showcased a
potpourri of perennial favorites and new tunes. The
first film to make it to the silver screen, *Easter Parade,*
paired Berlin's favorite performer, Fred Astaire, with
Judy Garland in a recasting of the Pygmalion-Galatea

myth. Along with the much-recycled song "Easter Parade" in the grand finale, the 1948 musical introduced "A Couple of Swells," which Astaire and Garland sang while cavorting as tramps.

Another new number in the show started out as a secret. As Garland struck a dancing pose with Berlin for publicity shots, she quipped, "Maybe this will inspire one of the new songs." Berlin laughed, slipped her a piece of paper, and swore her to secrecy. Garland glanced at the paper, which read, "It only happens when I dance with you." This was the title of *Easter Parade*'s new romantic ballad.

Powerful MGM boss Louis B. Mayer called *Easter Parade* "the *Gone with the Wind* of musicals." Berlin himself said of the movie: "Personally, I feel it's the most satisfactory musical I've ever been connected with. I'm sure it will be a tremendous success." The film captured an Academy Award for best scoring of a musical.

The next movie musical did not come off as smoothly. It was a movie version of *Annie Get Your Gun.* Judy Garland, who was so luminescent as the ingenue in *Easter Parade,* was slated to star as Annie Oakley. However, the young actress suffered from a series of emotional problems compounded by her increasing reliance on drugs. She had first been given amphetamines by MGM to help her lose weight when she was still a child. By 1950, she was hooked in a vicious cycle of pills to pep her up, calm her down, help her sleep, and control her weight. Exhausted, suicidal, and undergoing electroshock "therapy," Garland was unable to perform at her usual standard. MGM eventually fired Garland, even though she had already recorded the entire soundtrack. They also had to fire director Busby Berkeley. Compounding the calamity, the actor portraying Frank Butler broke his leg, and the one playing Buffalo Bill died.

Filming resumed once a new director was hired, and actress Betty Hutton replaced Garland. Although late and over budget, *Annie Get Your Gun* was a success when finally released, and it won Berlin another Oscar for adaptation scoring. The spirited Hollywood production showcased Berlin's songs with a bull's-eye precision.

Meanwhile, Berlin busied himself on the opposite coast writing songs for *Miss Liberty,* a Broadway musical about the Statue of Liberty. This production also proved problematic. Robert Sherwood, a prominent playwright, based part of *Miss Liberty's* plot on the beautiful French girl who had posed for the statue. Problem was, Berlin discovered, the sculptor's mother actually modeled for the Statue of Liberty. Sherwood rewrote the story while Berlin composed songs personifying the national icon that had welcomed him to America so many years before. He even set Emma Lazarus's famous poem honoring the statue to music with the song "Give Me Your Tired, Your Poor."

Sherwood and Berlin put up the money to produce the show themselves. When *Miss Liberty* made its Broadway debut in 1949, Berlin said he felt "good about this thing. But a fellow never can tell. He works hard fixing up a lot of dishes he's sure are all good. But when the theatre-goer sits down to them and gets to dessert he may have indigestion—or worse."

Miss Liberty proved unpalatable to theatergoers and critics, and faded from the stage in a few months. This time, not one of Berlin's new songs became a hit.

Chapter Eight

Counting His Blessings

Berlin once admitted he would not want to continue working if his talent was gone. He also knew it would be difficult to know when that happened. "Who is going to tell me that I'm washed up as a songwriter? That day is sure to come, and I'm always afraid my friends won't have the courage to tell me. I don't want to make my exit in the midst of a bunch of mediocre songs. I want my last one to have just as much merit as the first."

When his mediocre musical *Miss Liberty* closed, the songwriter began work on a new stage show in hopes of restoring his reputation. This time around, the play he scored was inspired by a contemporary figure named Perle Mesta, a Washington socialite President Truman had named ambassador to Luxembourg. It was a fish-out-of-water scenario that seemed ripe with comic possibilities, especially with brash Ethel Merman starring as the ambassador. There was a war going on in Korea and a musical comedy poking fun at politics seemed a good venue for Berlin to base his comeback on.

While Berlin worked on songs for *Call Me Madam,* a number he had written back in 1914 reappeared on the hit parade. The double song "Play a Simple Melody" enjoyed fresh success when sung as "Simple Melody" by Bing Crosby and his son Gary. When the second act of *Call Me Madam* bogged down during pre-Broadway tryouts, Merman asked for new song like "Simple Melody" that she could sing with the show's juvenile lead, Russell Nype. She had noticed the applause that Nype, who played her Ivy League aide, got when he sang "It's a Lovely Day Today." Merman told Berlin, "I want a duet with the kid!"

Berlin hid out in his hotel room for two days and banged on the black note keys of his Buick. When he emerged, he was carrying the sheet music for "(You're Not Sick) You're Just in Love." "It's nice after all these years to know that you can still reach up there and find it when you're in trouble," he later said about the piece. After rehearsing the song with Nype, Merman predicted, "We'll never get off the stage." *Call Me Madam* opened at New York's Imperial Theater October 12,

1950. It sold more than a million dollars in tickets before it even opened. Top tickets fetched $7.20—the highest ever on Broadway. Both Merman and Nype went on to win Tony Awards for their performances.

The show had some of Berlin's most memorable songs. He coined another new phrase with "The Hostess with the Mostes' on the Ball." "They Like Ike," in honor of his friend General Eisenhower, became the first in a series of "Ike" songs. Four years later, President Eisenhower would host the Berlins at the White House, where he announced that a Congressional Gold

President Dwight D. Eisenhower and First Lady Mamie Eisenhower present Irving Berlin with the Congressional Gold Medal. *(Courtesy of The Estate of Irving Berlin.)*

Irving Berlin was the second songwriter in history to receive the Congressional Gold Medal. The first was George M. Cohan, who served as an inspiration to Berlin. *(Courtesy of The Estate of Irving Berlin.)*

Medal would be struck honoring Berlin's contributions to American popular song with "God Bless America." After receiving splendid reviews, *Call Me Madam* racked up 644 performances.

Even an old adversary named Brooks Atkinson, a critic for the *New York Times,* gave it a glowing review. "After forty-five years on the sidewalks of Tin Pan Alley, Mr. Berlin is entitled to lose some of his rapture and enthusiasm. He doesn't. He has bestowed on *Call Me Madam* one of his most delightful cornucopias of sound." *Call Me Madam*, Atkinson concluded, "throws a little stardust around the theatre and sets the audience to roaring."

When the show closed on Broadway, a national tour and two London productions were staged and Merman reprised her role in the film version of *Call Me Madam.* Her strong contralto rang out on Berlin's 1913 song "That International Rag," which was added to the movie and became a hit all over again in 1953.

More Berlin classics could be heard on the silver screen in two 1954 films. *White Christmas* featured the evergreen title song in a plot about two song-and-dance men and a sister act who help an old army general save his Vermont inn. Berlin's chronic insomnia inspired another catchy song from the film called "Count Your Blessings Instead of Sheep."

He said about this number, "Some time ago, after the

Ethel Merman and Irving Berlin on the set of *There's No Business Like Show Business*. *(Courtesy of The Estate of Irving Berlin.)*

worst kind of a sleepless night, my doctor came to see me, and after a lot of self-pity . . . he looked at me and said, 'Speaking of doing something about insomnia, did you ever try counting your blessings?' " This 1954 song would be the composer's last bona fide hit from his song catalog.

Berlin continued to work. *There's No Business Like Show Business* developed a story around the title song and included a large number of the composer's popular tunes in a somewhat confusing tale of a vaudeville family. The movie featured two new attractions to lure in viewers. It was filmed in CinemaScope, a recently developed wide-screen system using curved screens, and spotlighted a new star named Marilyn Monroe, who sang "Heat Wave." This torch song had been sung on screen before in 1933's *As Thousands Cheer.*

The recycling of his old songs emphasized just how far back Berlin was reaching to score his new musicals. He nearly emptied his trunk of songs. *There's No Business Like Show Business* was his last movie score.

Chapter Nine

Out of Tune

During the 1950s, popular music experienced another transformation. By the end of the decade, the new rock and roll filled the radio airwaves. The spotlight shifted from the songwriter to the song singer and many of the new performers, both solo and groups, either wrote their own songs or worked closely with a small circle of writers. Jazz, which Berlin had borrowed from over the years, became more "modern," with dissonant sounds and difficult chord changes and a heightened emphasis on instrumental virtuosity over melody.

Berlin tried to compete with the new music. Concerning Berlin's 1955 song, "Aesop (That Able Fable Man)," a columnist for the *New York Journal-American* commented, "Irving Berlin has written—are you ready—a bop song. It's about Aesop, and it's sure to make the juke boxes jingle."

The same publication predicted "Irving Berlin's irrepressible energy has him back on Tin Pan Alley, batting out candidates for the hit parade. The first to make the juke boxes will be 'Out of This World into My Arms'—and the disc artists are scrambling to record it."

It was not to be, however. Neither song became a hit. The gap continued to widen between the older Tin Pan Alley composers and the new music, particularly rock and roll. Berlin had always exercised tight creative control over his songs. Then Elvis Presley released his 1957 *Christmas Album*, featuring Berlin's "White Christmas." Horrified over Presley's rock and roll rendition, Berlin attempted to have radio stations across the country yank the song from airplay.

It was all to no avail. A new note in popular music had sounded, and the songwriter was out of tune. He decided to retire. He had been working since age eight and it was time to learn how to relax.

Retiring was easier said than done. Berlin discovered he had no talent for relaxing. He first tried to stay at his Catskill estate and fish for trout in the solitude of a mountain stream. Then he transformed his Lew Beach teahouse into an artist studio, where he painted bowls of flowers along with other still lifes and portraits. He gave Bing Crosby and Fred Astaire paintings. He even painted what he referred to as a self-portrait—a cow in a meadow.

Through it all, Berlin thought about songwriting. "As a painter, I'm a pretty good songwriter," he lamented. The year of his retirement, 1958, marked the first time in fifty years that no new Berlin songs were copyrighted. The royalties from his old songs continued to roll in, but his Buick gathered dust.

He later reflected upon this attempt at retirement. "I wrote no music, I made no songs. I idled. For five years, first, health troubles. Nerves, ague pains, twitches. Then depression. I got to the point I didn't want to leave my room when daylight came."

Irving Berlin took up painting during retirement and gave a number of his works to colleagues and celebrities, including Fred Astaire. *(Courtesy of The Estate of Irving Berlin.)*

Unlike the title of his 1953 tune, the songwriter was not content "Sittin' in the Sun, Countin' My Money." Retirement, Berlin realized, "made me sick. I mean that. I got really sick. I suffered severe bouts of depression. I worried about everything when, really, I had nothing to worry about. It takes a very rare person to retire gracefully if he has been a success . . . I had no hobbies . . . My only hobby is songwriting. So I went back to work." He offered this advice: "Every man with any kind of talent look at me and heed—don't quit, don't turn your back on the mystery of talent, don't abandon what was given to you, don't scorn your gifts. Use them until your last day on earth and live a full, rich and rewarding life."

Berlin returned to Broadway at the age of seventy-four with a new musical, *Mr. President*. It was an attempt to capture the vigor and charm of the young president John F. Kennedy. The songs were full of patriotic energy. "*Mr. President* is all about America. But put it this way: while we take a lot of things lightly, we take America seriously," Berlin said. "You can't sell patriotism unless people feel patriotic. For that matter, you can't sell people anything they don't want."

It seemed a patriotic musical was just the ticket for American audiences. Before the show went on the boards in October 1962, advance ticket sales reached above the $2.5-million mark, guaranteeing a lengthy run.

As the songs for *Mr. President* took shape, Berlin flashed back to the patriotism expressed in "God Bless America." The song, Berlin wrote, "is simple, honest— a patriotic statement. It's an emotion, not just words and music. A patriotic song *is* an emotion, and you must not embarrass an audience with it, or they'll hate your guts. It has to be right, and the time for it has to be right."

At the Washington premiere of *Mr. President,* the president and first lady bought every seat at the National Theatre. The proceeds were used to benefit their favorite charities. The stage was set for a spectacle and a grand night for the audience and the composer. The premiere was soured, however, when President Kennedy delayed his arrival until a televised boxing match was over, and then left before the final curtain call. Apparently, other audience members wished they could follow suit. Instead of revitalizing Berlin's music, *Mr. President* flopped. The corny songs and mediocre plot guaranteed this would be his final Broadway musical.

Berlin became involved in a bizarre lawsuit against *Mad,* the humor magazine targeting a young audience. *Mad* had published a sing-along issue poking fun at "57 old standards which reflect the idiotic world we live in today." Many of the songs parodied were Berlin classics. An infuriated Berlin sued the magazine, although neither his music nor lyrics had appeared in its pages.

Berlin had gotten his own start writing parodies of popular songs in the early 1900s; a half century later, he found others doing the same thing to be libelous. At least his attorney kept his sense of humor. He quipped *Mad* had committed "Piracy on the High C's."

The lawsuit did have serious ramifications. The First Amendment to the United States Constitution states, "Congress shall make no law . . . abridging the freedom . . . of the press." If Berlin, who had joined together with other music publishers in the suit, won, the freedom to write parodies of anyone's music or other works would have vanished. In the final decision, Judge Irving R. Kaufman ruled in favor of *Mad*. "We doubt that even so eminent a composer as Irving Berlin should be permitted to claim a proprietary interest in iambic pentameter," he scolded in his decision.

Berlin had struck several sour notes recently, but he hoped harmony was on the horizon. Encouraged by the success of Broadway's *Fiddler on the Roof*, he dusted off his unfinished *East River*, a musical about immigrant life on the Lower East Side.

Although Berlin now lived most of the time at a fashionable Upper East Side address, he often visited the streets where he had grown up as Israel Beilin. Through the windows of his Beekman Place townhouse he could glimpse the East River. "I've always lived near this river, ever since I came to New York. It's like completing a circle." His *East River* musical, however, was never completed.

In 1963, producer Arthur Freed announced MGM had coaxed Berlin back to Hollywood to create "the greatest musical ever made." The timing seemed ripe as the songwriter had recently won the Screen Producers Guild Milestone Award for "historic contributions to movies." The multimillion dollar musical, *Say It with Music,* would combine new songs with fifty years of Berlin standards. Since the songwriter, through Irving Berlin, Inc., owned the copyrights to his entire song catalog, he could showcase his tunes without a hitch.

Agent Irving P. (Swifty) Lazar recalled Berlin playing a medley of new tunes created for *Say It with Music*: "The way Berlin sold a song was unique. He would lean his face within an inch of yours and sing it to you. Well, he sang the song and some others and Freed bought the score for a million dollars. He was the first to sell a score for a million."

The budget for *Say It with Music* quickly swelled to fifteen million dollars. A revolving door of high-priced stars was slated to star. At various times during the production, the roster included Judy Garland, Ethel Merman, Frank Sinatra, Fred Astaire, Bing Crosby, Johnny Mathis, Julie Andrews, and Sophia Loren, with Vincente Minnelli directing and Jerome Robbins choreographing.

The Ed Sullivan Show held a star-studded celebration in honor of Irving Berlin's eightieth birthday. *(Courtesy of The Estate of Irving Berlin.)*

The project was cursed with casting troubles, bad scripts, corporate battles for control of MGM, and internal studio politics. In the face of the chaos, Berlin optimistically penned ten new songs, including "I Used to Play It by Ear."

As he waited for *Say It with Music* to start filming, *Annie Get Your Gun* enjoyed a revival. The 1966 version played at swanky Lincoln Center in Manhattan, and once again starred Ethel Merman as Annie Oakley. Berlin penned another double song: "An Old-Fashioned Wedding," which stopped the show. The revival was a hit both on Broadway and on its road tour.

In May of 1968, Ed Sullivan devoted his ninety-minute television variety show to celebrating Berlin's eightieth birthday. President Lyndon Johnson made a surprise appearance to congratulate America's musical laureate, saying, "America is the richer for his presence. God Bless Berlin." Bob Hope, Bing Crosby, Ethel Merman, and the Motown group The Supremes all paid tribute. Singer Robert Goulet premiered Berlin's newest song, "I Used to Play It by Ear." Then Berlin took the stage, capping off the evening by leading Boy and Girl Scouts in a rendition of "God Bless America."

The song had an encore performance on his actual birthday, May 11, at a special Central Park celebration. A children's marching band paraded before the convertible carrying Berlin and Ellin to the section of the park called Sheep Meadow. About eight thousand Girl Scouts serenaded the songwriter with "Happy Birthday." Berlin joined the scouts in singing "God Bless America."

During a promotion for the Sullivan show, Berlin modestly called "God Bless America" a "very ordinary patriotic song that any child could have written. 'Land that I love'—what child couldn't write that? It was the timing that counted." However, it was not a good time for patriotism as the 1960s progressed. Antiwar songs, not tributes to America, ruled the airwaves. Berlin even penned a special version of "God Bless America" for one of his lyric writer friends, Edgar Y. Harburg, in 1969. Harburg, born of Russian-Jewish immigrant parents on the Lower East Side, had penned lyrics to more than five hundred songs, including "Brother, Can You Spare a Dime," an unofficial anthem of the Great Depression, and "Over the Rainbow" for *The Wizard of Oz*.

The two songwriters' politics could not have been more different. Harburg's left-wing politics led to him being blacklisted in Hollywood during the postwar red scare that consumed Hollywood and Washington. In 1947, the House Un-American Activities Committee labeled the lyrics of "And Russia Is Her Name" as pro-Communist. However, Berlin and Harburg respected each other and lived with their political differences. Berlin joked his parody could be called "God Help America" using the same tune.

The entertainment industry had also radically changed by 1969. Film musicals no longer drew big audiences. Popular music by the Beatles and other rock and roll performers blared from radios and record shops. Although Berlin admired such Beatles' tunes as "Yesterday" and "Michelle," he had no desire to emulate them at this stage in his career. "Who cares anymore?

There's a whole new public out there, and they don't even know people like me are still around," Berlin realized. "We're antiques, museum pieces. Today, it's all kids."

Finally, the new boss at MGM took a look at the bloated budget for *Say It with Music* and terminated the musical. The end of Berlin's Hollywood songwriting career eerily echoed the beginning, when the songs were yanked from his 1930 film *Reaching for the Moon*. Only this time he would not dispel his disappointment with new hits.

Years later, Berlin reflected on his inability to keep in tune with the new generation of American popular music. "It was as if I owned a store and people no longer wanted to buy what I had to sell." He realized that everything had changed. "The world was a different place. The death of President Kennedy, the Vietnam War, the social protest. Music changed, too. The Beatles and other groups reached audiences. I couldn't. It was time to close up shop."

This time, Berlin went into permanent retirement. As the music stopped, the man who had been known as Mister Music gradually became a recluse. He even donated his battered Buick to the Smithsonian Institution. "That's the proper place for it now that I'm no longer writing songs," Berlin said.

Chapter Ten

The Melody Lingers

Throughout the last two decades of his life, the retired songwriter collected royalties as new artists recorded his songs and old versions continued to play on the radio. Berlin received several tempting offers to sell the rights to his songs, even his entire catalog, but always refused. Director Steven Spielberg, for example, attempted to negotiate the rights to "Always" to be used in his movie of the same title. Each time the songwriter refused, Spielberg upped the ante. The bidding continued until Berlin, who was in his late nineties, confessed he had future plans for the song.

Although Berlin had officially retired, he occasionally returned to composing. "Song for the U.N.," his final published song, premiered at the annual United Nations concert and dinner in Washington, D.C. in October of 1971. The event marked the U.N.'s twenty-fifth anniversary. It was billed as both "A Birthday Toast to the United Nations" and "A Tribute to Irving Berlin, Songwriter to the World."

The world's songwriter wrote, "Through the years, I've been asked many times to write a peace song but always decided it just couldn't be done. You will see when you read the lyrics that the song is *about* a peace song that hasn't been written yet. Note the five words, 'One song with one word.' Even as 'great' a songwriter as I couldn't possibly write a song with one word." The word was "peace."

Two years later, he sang "God Bless America," at a White House dinner honoring returning American prisoners of war from Vietnam. This was Berlin's last public appearance.

In January 1977, President Gerald R. Ford presented Berlin the highest civilian award, the Presidential Medal of Freedom, which is given to individuals who make significant contributions to the "quality of American life." Berlin was honored for his patriotic contributions during the two world wars.

A private person, Berlin slipped out of the spotlight. When new plays debuted at the Music Box, he was not in the audience. He rarely left his house, preferring to keep in touch with old theater friends and check on song royalties through the telephone.

His disappearance from the scene breathed new life into an old rumor that Irving Berlin was an invention, a front for several songwriters, as surely, no single human could have written all those songs.

On the hundredth anniversary of the Statue of Liberty, in 1986, it seemed fitting that the songwriter who had penned *Miss Liberty* be honored. Berlin was one of twelve naturalized Americans who received the Liberty Medal from President Ronald Reagan. The songwriter did not attend the Liberty Weekend celebration, preferring to watch it on television. Later, PBS broadcasted a television documentary, *Irving Berlin's America,* to mark the occasion.

Two years later, another milestone was marked when Irving Berlin turned one hundred. Among the many tributes he received was a star-studded performance of his music at Carnegie Hall on May 11, 1988. Berlin's three daughters and several of his nine grandchildren attended the benefit concert hosted by ASCAP. Newscaster Walter Cronkite began the evening by listing Berlin's hits. Then stars such as Shirley MacLaine, Leonard Bernstein, Natalie Cole, and Frank Sinatra performed a sampling of songs during the three-hour tribute. Essayist Garrison Keillor said Berlin had taken "common American talk, our talk, and turned it into poetry." Then he proved his point by reciting the lyrics to "All Alone," which he described as an eighty-one-word poem without a single unnecessary word.

For the grand finale, the Carnegie Hall stage filled with the United States Army Chorus, who sang "This Is the Army," followed by Girl and Boy Scouts singing "God Bless America." The songwriter celebrated his century of life at home with Ellin, dining in their flower-filled library.

Berlin was treated to a special, private birthday performance without having to leave his Beekman Place home. Friends serenaded him from the sidewalk with "Happy Birthday" and "Always."

A few months later, his beloved Ellin, the inspiration behind "Always" and several other of his best songs, died. At her funeral mass, Cardinal John O'Connor praised Berlin's wife by saying, "No man could have given the joy to the world that Irving Berlin gave had he not had the love and support of a wonderful woman."

Berlin grieved the loss of his wife, but he did not wait long before joining her. On September 22, 1989, at the age of 101, Irving Berlin died in his sleep. He was buried beside Ellin at Woodlawn Cemetery in the Bronx. When a reporter asked if the songwriter had been ill, Berlin's son-in-law replied, "No. He was a hundred and one years old. He just fell asleep." At the time of his death, Berlin was survived by three daughters, nine grandchildren, and six great-grandchildren.

President George Bush issued a statement the following day.

> I was saddened to hear of the death of Irving Berlin. Very few composers have come to touch the soul of a nation, reflecting its spirit and traditions. Mr. Berlin ranks among such composers, having become a living legend in his own lifetime. His love of country and fellow man, so vividly demonstrated in his songs, were characteristics which we all admired and which will be part of his legacy. His songs, such as 'God Bless America' and 'White Christmas,' have become woven into the very fabric of American society, touching the lives of generations of Americans.

Berlin's three daughters, along with ASCAP, staged a memorial tribute to the songwriter in 1990 at his Music Box Theatre, which continues to feature Broadway productions. New York's theater district also hosted reunions of soldiers who had starred in Berlin's World War II musical, *This Is the Army.*

In her book, *Irving Berlin: A Daughter's Memoir,* eldest daughter Mary Ellin Barrett wrote, "There were periods when my father was convinced he would be forgotten, that it was a laugh to think people would sing his songs in the next century." On this Berlin was wrong. His music is still played and heard in venues all over America.

Berlin's name was once again in lights on Broadway when *Annie Get Your Gun* returned to the stage, starring Bernadette Peters in 1999, and country music star Reba McEntire in 2001. The Berlin songs, McEntire told *Billboard,* "have such a 'character arc' in each one, which lets me take a roller coaster ride each time I sing them. Someone said, 'I didn't know Irving Berlin wrote country songs!' But they certainly fit me to a 'T.' They're timeless, marvelous, funny, intriguing."

Berlin's pieces are still used in new Hollywood films—"Cheek to Cheek" in the Oscar winner *The English Patient,* as well as in *Any Given Sunday, Out to Sea,* and *Down to Earth.* "Puttin' on the Ritz" appears in *Young Frankenstein. Home Alone* features "White Christmas." *The Associate* contains "There's No Business Like Show Business." "Let's Face the Music and Dance" pops up in *Let It Be Me.* "All Alone" can be heard in *Sleepers. Billy Elliot* spotlights "Top Hat."

"White Christmas," Berlin's ultimate hit pop song, remains, as he once bragged, a publishing business in itself. With 125 million copies recorded by hundreds of artists in dozens of languages (including Yiddish), "White Christmas" continues its reign as the world's top-selling song. At the turn of the twenty-first century, new renditions were recorded by Destiny's Child, U2, Kiss, Barry Manilow, Gloria Estefan, Michael Bolton, Garth Brooks, and the Backstreet Boys.

Records have given way to audiotapes and compact discs, but a wide range of musical artists continue to record Berlin's tunes. The eclectic recordings include Natalie Cole's "Let's Face the Music and Dance," Taco's "Puttin' on the Ritz," Patsy Cline's "Always," Willie Nelson's "Blue Skies," K.T. Oslin's "I'll See You in C.U.B.A.," Aretha Franklin's "Say It Isn't So," Linda Ronstadt's "What'll I Do?" and Fun Boy Three's reggae version of "Let's Face the Music and Dance."

When the National Endowment for the Arts and the Recording Industry Association of America unveiled what they judged to be the top 365 songs of the twentieth century, four Berlin songs made the list. "Alexander's Ragtime Band" came in at 154, "Puttin' on the Ritz" at 117, "God Bless America" at nineteen, and "White Christmas" at two.

Perhaps the nineteenth song should have been bumped up to first place after the September 11, 2001, terrorist attacks on the World Trade Center in New York and the Pentagon in Washington, D.C. "God Bless America" provided comfort to Americans in the wake of the tragedy when senators and members of Congress sang it on the Capitol steps in Washington, D.C. Broadway casts lead theatergoers in singing it. The U.S. Army Orchestra played it at the National Cathedral in Washington during an official requiem. When the New York Stock Exchange reopened, New York Governor George

Pataki and Mayor Rudolph Giuliani joined traders in singing it. It became the theme song of the seventh-inning stretch at Major League Baseball games.

Citizens from coast to coast spontaneously sang America's unofficial national anthem to express their feelings of patriotism. Record shops reported a run on Kate Smith albums including the song. Everyone came together to embrace Berlin's "God Bless America"—a hit all over again, eighty-three years after it was written.

' "God Bless America' " evokes a sense of unity and calm," explained Berlin's daughter Linda Emmet. She continued:

> 'Stand beside her and guide her through the night with a light from above.' What happened on September 11 could metaphorically be the night; the light could be our continuing to move on. I know my father would be proud that, to this day, his song still stirs and bonds us. If the world doesn't suddenly blow itself up, I think people one hundred or two hundred years from now will still be singing it.

Irving Berlin is again a household name. His Buick remains on display at the Smithsonian Institution in Washington, D.C. Visitors are amazed at how this transposing piano allowed instant changes of key in an era long before computerized keyboards made it possible. "America's music," violinist Isaac Stern once said, "was born at his piano." The Smithsonian's National Portrait Gallery also offers a variety of musical shows and slide lectures spotlighting Berlin's music.

Nearby, American Treasures at the Library of Congress features the Irving Berlin Collection, which Berlin's three daughters donated in 1992. The remarkable collection includes personal papers, scrapbooks, and records of the Irving Berlin Music Corp. Original printer's proof and manuscript and lyric sheets for "God Bless America" are part of the collection. These detail the song's step-by-step evolution.

The Rodgers and Hammerstein Archives of Recorded Sound of the New York Public Library offer one of the richest resources of recorded sound in the world. Visitors can listen to rare recordings of Irving Berlin singing his own songs. A recent anthology, "Irving Sings Berlin," features the songwriter performing songs ranging from an early pre-World War I recording to a demo from 1962's *Mr. President.*

In 2002, Irving Berlin was commemorated on a U.S. postage stamp that was first dedicated at a special ceremony in Times Square, New York, on September 15, during the annual outdoor "Broadway on Broadway" concert that kicks off the new theater season. After one of Berlin's daughters and granddaughters unveiled the stamp, the entire crowd of fifteen thousand spectators sang "God Bless America" in a stirring tribute to the man and the song. The stamp, based on a colorized photograph of the songwriter taken by photographer Edward Steichen in 1932, is superimposed over a fragment of Berlin's handwritten score of "God Bless America." Berlin's signature appears across the bottom.

For someone who so profoundly influenced American music, Berlin always modestly claimed that he had created only five "key" songs, which he continuously recycled. "The five most important songs I ever wrote, structurally," he once revealed, "were 'Alexander's Ragtime Band,' 'Everybody Step,' 'What'll I Do?, 'A Pretty Girl Is Like a Melody,' and 'Cheek to Cheek.' " His musical fingerprints, however, are all over American popular songs to this day.

Major Songs

1907—Marie From Sunny
Italy
1908—Dorando
1909—My Wife's Gone to
the Country (Hur-
rah! Hurrah!)
1910—Oh, That Beautiful
Rag
1911—Alexander's Ragtime
Band
Everybody's Doin' It
Now
1912—When I Lost You
1913—That International Rag
1914—Play a Simple Melody
1915—I Love a Piano
1918—Oh! How I Hate to Get
Up in the Morning

God Bless America
(original)
1919—You'd Be Surprised
A Pretty Girl Is Like a
Melody
1921—Say It with Music
1922—Pack Up Your Sins
(and Go to the
Devil)
Everybody Step
1924—What'll I Do?
All Alone
1925—Always
1926—Russian Lullaby
1926—Blue Skies
1930—Let Me Sing and I'm
Happy
Puttin' on the Ritz

1932—Let's Have Another Cup of Coffee
How Deep Is the Ocean?
I Don't Wanna Be Married, I Just Wanna Be Friends
I Say It's Spinach
Say It Isn't So
1933—Man Bites Dog
Heat Wave
Supper Time
Easter Parade
1935—Cheek to Cheek
Isn't This a Lovely Day?
Top Hat, White Tie and Tails
1936—Let's Face the Music and Dance
I'm Putting All My Eggs in One Basket
1938—God Bless America (revised)
Change Partners
1940—Fools Fall in Love
It's a Lovely Day Tomorrow
1942—Abraham
Be Careful, It's My Heart
Let's Say It with Fire-crackers
Plenty to Be Thankful For

Let's Start the New Year Right
White Christmas
1946—You Can't Get a Man with a Gun
Doin' What Comes Natur'lly
Anything You Can Do
There's No Business Like Show Business
I Got Lost in His Arms
1947—The Freedom Train
1948—A Couple of Swells
Better Luck Next Time
It Only Happens When I Dance with You
1949—Give Me Your Tired, Your Poor
1950—It's a Lovely Day Today
(You're Not Sick) You're Just in Love
The Hostess with the Mostes' on the Ball
They Like Ike
1954—Count Your Blessings Instead of Sheep
1955—Aesop (That Able Fable Man)
1963—I Used to Play It by Ear
1966—An Old-Fashioned Wedding
1971—Song for the U.N.

Timeline

1888   May 11, Israel Beilin, better known as Irving Berlin, is born in Siberia, Russia.

1893   Irving and his family travel by steamship to America and settle in the Lower East Side of New York.

1901   Father dies.

1907   Irving's first work, "Marie from Sunny Italy" is published with first appearance of his last name as Berlin.

1909   Hired by Waterson & Snyder as an in-house lyricist.

1912   Becomes a partner at his music publishing company, now known as Waterson, Berlin & Snyder; marries Dorothy Goetz; five months later, Dorothy dies of typhoid fever.

1918   Becomes a citizen of the United States; drafted into the army during World War I; writes and stages *Yip, Yip, Yaphank*.

1919   Establishes his own music publishing firm, Irving Berlin, Inc.; Irving Berlin week takes place across America.

1924 Meets Ellin Mackay.

1926 Berlin and Mackay elope, despite opposition from her father and friends.

1929 Berlin loses his fortune in the stock market crash of October 29.

1938 Public hears "God Bless America" for the first time on Kate Smith's radio show.

1942 Writes "White Christmas," the best selling Christmas song of all time; writes and stages *This is the Army* to raise money for the Army Emergency Relief Fund.

1958 Attempts to retire.

1968 Celebrates his eightieth birthday on *The Ed Sullivan Show*.

1977 Receives Presidential Medal of Freedom from President Gerald R. Ford.

1988 Turns one hundred years old.

1989 Irving Berlin dies at age 101.

Sources

CHAPTER ONE: "On the Bum"

p. 13, "I never felt poverty . . ." *New York Sun,* February 24, 1947.

p. 14, "I was a little Russian . . ." *Saturday Evening Post,* January 14, 1944.

p. 16, "He just dreams . . ." Michael Freedland, *A Salute to Irving Berlin* (Santa Barbara, CA: Landmark Books, 1986), 12.

p. 17, "Aside from singing in schul . . ." Ibid., 13.

p. 19, "I always think of my youth . . ." *New York World-Telegram,* November 6, 1941.

p. 22, "I never wanted to be a songwriter . . ." Robert Kimball and Linda Emmet, eds. *The Complete Lyrics of Irving Berlin* (New York: Alfred A. Knopf, 2001), 4.

CHAPTER TWO: Making the Country Hum

p. 26, "Three-fourths of that . . ." *Melody Maker,* November 6, 1954.

p. 27, "The Man Who . . ." *New York World,* July 10, 1910.

p. 27, "Song writing all depends . . ." Ibid.

p. 27, "The black keys are . . ." *New York Press,* December 20, 1914.

p. 29, "I sacrifice one . . ." *Green Book Magazine,* February 1915.

p. 30, "I wrote it without words . . ." *New York Post,* July 14, 1938.

p. 32, "was very swell for me." *New York Sun,* February 24, 1947.

CHAPTER THREE: The Hit Maker

p. 34, "You certainly have . . ." David Ewen, *The Story of Irving Berlin* (New York: Henry Holt and Company, 1950), 73.

p. 34, "I write words and music . . ." Kimball, *Lyrics of Irving Berlin*, 40.

p. 35, "The reason our American . . ." *Theatre Magazine,* February 1915.

p. 36, "He was my inspiration . . ." Freedland, *Salute to Irving Berlin*, 59.

p. 37, "I'm through, finished . . ." Ewen, *Story of Irving Berlin,* 78.

p. 37, "He [Berlin] has written a score . . ." David Ewen, *Great Men of American Popular Song*, (Englewood Cliffs, NJ: Prentice-Hall, Inc. 1970), 107.

p. 38, "You write in the morning . . ." Ibid., 115.

p. 38, "when the phrase of melody . . ." Ibid., 114.

p. 39, "The reason I write simply . . ." Edward Jablonski, *Irving Berlin: American Troubadour* (New York: Henry Holt and Company, 1999), 287.

p. 39, "I tried to learn how . . ." *New York Times,* October 14, 1962.

p. 40, "I wrote more lousy songs . . ." Kimball, *Lyrics of Irving Berlin*, xvi.

p. 40, "Frankly, there are some songs . . ." Groucho Marx, *The Groucho Letters* (New York: Simon & Schuster, 1967), 210-211.

p. 41, "Oh, Mr. Berlin . . ." Alexander Woollcott, *The Story of Irving Berlin* (New York: G.P. Putman's Sons, 1925), 151.

p. 42, "There were a lot . . ." *American Heritage,* August 1967.

p. 42, "The other soldiers . . ." Ibid.

p. 43, "See, there were so many . . ." Max Wilk, *They're Playing Our Song,* (New York: Atheneum, 1973), 276.

p. 44, "It seemed a little like . . ." Freedland, *Salute to Irving Berlin*, 126.

p. 44, "I have heard . . ." *Variety,* August 23, 1918.

CHAPTER FOUR: New Music for New Action

p. 43, "I can't get to work . . ." *Theater Magazine*, February 1915.

p. 47, "It was the age of the automobile . . ." Freedland, *A Salute to Irving Berlin*, 69.

p. 47, "too much Berlin" Ibid., 89.

p. 49, "Usually, writing songs . . ." *Theater Magazine,* January 1916.

p. 49, "It has always been assumed . . ." Freedland, *Salute to Irving Berlin*, 105.

p. 50, "With grammar, I can . . ." Jablonski, *American Troubadour*, 106.

p. 50, "in a high, wispy, always . . ." Mary Ellin Barrett, *Irving Berlin: A Daughter's Memoir* (New York: Simon & Schuster, 1994), 24.

p. 50, "Modern girls are conscious . . ." *New Yorker,* December 1925.

p. 50, "I really am delighted . . ." Kimball, *Lyrics of Irving Berlin*, 211.

p. 51, "The only breath of salt air . . ." Ibid., 194.

p. 52, "I think I just heard . . ." Howard Teichman, *George S. Kaufman* (New York: Atheneum, 1972), 91.

p. 52, "have a musical without music" Jablonski, *American Troubadour*, 120.

CHAPTER FIVE: A Crack of Insecurity

p. 56, "Luckily I had a rich wife." Barrett, *A Daughter's Memoir*, 82.

p. 56, "I was scared . . ." *Saturday Evening Post,* January 9, 1943.

p. 56, "developed the damnedest . . ." Kimball, *Lyrics of Irving Berlin*, 266.

p. 56, "Musicals were the rage . . ." New York Times, May 11, 1958.

p. 57, "George took it down . . ." Deena Rosenberg, *Fascinating Rhythm: The Collaboration of George and Ira Gershwin* (New York: Dutton, 1991), 25.

p. 57, "Stick to your own songs . . ." Barrett, *A Daughter's Memoir*, 155.

p. 58, "It was a simple . . ." *New York Herald Tribune,* February 23, 1932.

p. 58, "We have become a world of listeners. . ." Philip Furia, *Irving Berlin: A Life in Song* (New York: Schirmer Books, 1998), 146.

p. 59, "Nowhere else in American . . ." Alec Wilder, *American Popular Music: The Great Innovators, 1900-1950* (New York: Oxford University Press, 1972), 108.

p. 60, "A song is like a marriage." *New York World Telegraph,* October 1, 1933.

CHAPTER SIX: God Bless America

p. 63, "I worked for a while . . ." *New York Times,* October 27, 1940.

p. 64, "hard to do, because . . ." *New York Journal American,* September 4, 1938.

p. 64, "one of the most beautiful . . ." Kimball, *Lyrics of Irving Berlin*, 321.

p. 65, "caught on because it happens . . ." *New York Times,* July 28, 1940.

p. 65, "All that I hope for . . ." Kimball, *Lyrics of Irving Berlin*, 322.

p. 66, "For the first time . . ." Barrett, *A Daughter's Memoir*, 168.

p. 67, "The public has been getting . . ." Ibid., 191.

p. 68, "We working composers . . ." *Saturday Evening Post,* January 14, 1944.

p. 69, "It came out at a time . . ." Freedland, *Salute to Irving Berlin*, 312.

p. 71, "There goes Time with your . . ." Barrett, *A Daughter's Memoir*, 233.

p. 72, "We always insisted that . . ." Laurence Bergreen, *As Thousands Cheer: The Life of Irving Berlin* (New York: Da Capo Press, Inc., 1996), 412.

p. 73, "It's the biggest emotional . . ." Freedland, *Salute to Irving Berlin*, 332.

p. 73, "If the guy who wrote . . ." Ronald Reagan and Richard G. Hubler, *Where's the Rest of Me?* (New York: Karz Publishers, 1981), 121-122.

CHAPTER SEVEN: Show Business

p. 75, "Irving Berlin has no place . . ." The Rodgers & Hammerstein Organization website, Berlin biography, http://www.rnh.com/bios/index.html Downloaded March 5, 2003.

p. 76, "At my age . . ." Jablonski, *American Troubadour*, 247.

p. 76, "All that time . . ." Freedland, *Salute to Irving Berlin*, 384-385.

p. 78, "There was only one . . ." *Happy Talk*, The Rodgers & Hammerstein Organization, Volume 8, Issue 2.

p. 78, "All you have to do . . ." Kimball, *Lyrics of Irving Berlin*, 387.

p. 79, "I've always thought of myself . . ." *New York Times,* May 11, 1958.

p. 79, "Yeah. A good old-fashioned . . ." Jablonski, *American Troubadour*, 245.

p. 79, "Aren't we lucky . . ." Ibid., 243.

p. 79, "An American by choice . . ." Freedland, *Salute to Irving Berlin*, 388.

p. 80, "I got terribly excited . . ." Kimball, *Lyrics of Irving Berlin*, 406.

p. 80, "I can only say . . ." Ibid.

p. 81, "Maybe this will . . ." Jablonski, *American Troubadour*, 252.

p. 81, "the *Gone with the Wind* . . ." Kimball, *Lyrics of Irving Berlin*, 399.

p. 81, "Personally, I feel it's the . . ." Ibid.

p. 83, "good about this thing . . ." Ibid., 411.

CHAPTER EIGHT: Counting His Blessings

p. 84, "Who is going to tell me . . ." *St. Louis Star-Times,* December 20, 1942.

p. 85, "I want a duet . . ." The Rodgers & Hammerstein Theatre Library website, http://www3.rnh.com/theatre/showslevel3/madam/about.html Downloaded March 5, 2003.

p. 85, "It's nice after . . ." Barrett, *A Daughter's Memoir*, 262.

p. 85, "We'll never get . . ." Bob Thomas, *I Got Rhythm! The Ethel Merman Story* (New York: Putnam, 1985), 111.

p. 88, "After forty-five years on the sidewalks . . ." *New York Times,* October 13, 1950.

p. 89, "Some time ago . . ." Barrett, *A Daughter's Memoir*, 278.

CHAPTER NINE: Out of Tune

p. 92, "Irving Berlin has written . . ." Kimball, *Lyrics of Irving Berlin*, 462.

p. 92, "Irving Berlin's irrepressible energy . . ." Ibid., 463.

p. 93, "As a painter . . ." Jablonski, *American Troubadour*, 286.

p. 93, "I wrote no music . . ." *London Daily Express,* September 13, 1963.

p. 94, "made me sick . . ." Ibid.

p. 94, "every man with any kind of . . ." *Philadelphia Inquirer,* August 25, 1966.

p. 94, "*Mr. President* is all about . . ." Jablonski, *American Troubadour*, 296.

p. 95, "is simple, honest . . ." Ibid.

p. 95, "57 old standards . . ." *Mad Magazine*, 1961.

p. 96, "Piracy on the High C's" Freedland, *Salute to Irving Berlin*, 290.

p. 96, "We doubt that . . ." *New York Times,* March 24, 1964.

p. 97, "I've always lived . . ." Freedland, *Salute to Irving Berlin*, 208.

p. 97, "The way Berlin sold . . ." Jablonski, *American Troubadour*, 307.

p. 99, "America is the richer . . ." Ewen, *Great Men of American Popular Song*, 115.

p. 99, "very ordinary patriotic . . ." Jablonski, *American Troubadour*, 313.

p. 101, "Who cares anymore . . ." Wilk, *They're Playing Our Song*, 264.

p. 101, "It was as if I . . ." Kimball, *Lyrics of Irving Berlin*, xix.

p. 101, "The world was a . . ." Barrett, *A Daughter's Memoir*, 294-295.

p. 101, "That's the proper place . . ." Freedland, *Salute to Irving Berlin*, 490.

CHAPTER TEN: The Melody Lingers

p. 103, "Through the years . . ." Kimball, *Lyrics of Irving Berlin*, 494.

p. 104, "common American talk, our talk . . ." Jablonski, *American Trubadour*, 327.

p. 105, "No man could have . . ." Bergreen, *As Thousands Cheer*, 583.

p. 105, "No. He was a hundred . . ." *Variety,* September 27, 1989.

p. 106, "I was saddened to hear of the death . . ." George Bush Presidential Library and Museum website, http://bushlibrary.tamu.edu/papers/1989/89092301.html Downloaded March 12, 2003.

p. 106, "There were periods when . . ." Barrett, *A Daughter's Memoir*, 295.

p.107, "have such a 'character . . ." *Happy Talk,* Volume 8, Issue 3.

p. 109, "'God Bless America' evokes . . ." *USA Weekend,* October 26-28, 2001.

p. 109, "America's music . . ." The Rodgers & Hammerstein Organization website, http://www.rnh.com/bios/index.html Downloaded March 12, 2003.

p. 111, "The five most important . . ." *Sunday News,* September 7, 1947.

Bibliography

Barrett, Mary Ellin. *Irving Berlin: A Daughter's Memoir.* New York: Simon & Schuster, 1994.

Bergreen, Laurence. *As Thousands Cheer: The Life of Irving Berlin.* New York: Da Capo Press, Inc., 1996.

Ewen, David. *Great Men of American Popular Song.* Englewood Cliffs, NJ: Prentice-Hall, Inc., 1970.

———. *The Story of Irving Berlin.* New York: Henry Holt and Company, 1950.

Freedland, Michael. *A Salute to Irving Berlin.* Santa Barbara, CA: Landmark Books, 1986.

Furia, Philip. *Irving Berlin: A Life in Song.* New York: Schirmer Books, 1998.

Jablonski, Edward. *Irving Berlin: American Troubadour.* New York: Henry Holt and Company, 1999.

Kimball, Robert, and Linda Berlin Emmet, eds. *The Complete Lyrics of Irving Berlin.* New York: Alfred A. Knopf, 2001.

Mast, Gerald. *Can't Help Singing: The American Musical on Stage and Screen.* Woodstock, NY: The Overlook Press, Woodstock, NY, 1987.

Wilder, Alec. *American Popular Music: The Great Innovators, 1900-1950.* New York: Oxford University Press, 1972.

Woollcott, Alexander. *The Story of Irving Berlin.* New York: G.P. Putman's Sons, 1925.

Websites

The Rodgers and Hammerstein Organization:
Irving Berlin Biography
http://www.rnh.com/bios/index.html

Covers of Irving Berlin Sheet Music
http://www.melodylane.net/standards8.html

Irving Berlin's Transposing Piano
http://www.concertpitchpiano.com/TinPanAlley.html

Index